buddha bowls

For Felix and Mathew, mum & dad x

10 9 8 7

Pop Press, an imprint of Ebury Publishing,
20 Vauxhall Bridge Road,
London, SW1V 2SA

 Penguin
Random House
UK

Pop Press is part of the Penguin Random House group
of companies whose addresses can be found at global.
penguinrandomhouse.com

Text by Hannah Pemberton © Ebury Press 2018
Photography © The Kitchen Alchemist 2018

www.penguin.co.uk

First published by Pop Press in 2018

A CIP catalogue record for this book is available from the
British Library

Design: Louise Evans / Photography: The Kitchen
Alchemist / Project management: whitefox

ISBN 9781785036675

Printed and bound in Italy by Printer Trento Srl

Penguin Random House is committed to a sustainable
future for our business, our readers and our planet.
This book is made from Forest Stewardship Council®
certified paper.

MIX
Paper from
responsible sources
FSC® C018179

buddha bowls

GRAIN + GREEN + PROTEIN

POP PRESS

CONTENTS

DRESSINGS & SAUCES

MORNING BOWLS

LUNCH BOWLS

EVENING BOWLS

WHAT IS A BUDDHA BOWL?

Mealtimes are about taking time out, for you and for your body.

But you don't always want to spend hours in the kitchen, and if you opt for a plant-based diet, it can be tough to know whether you're eating a perfectly balanced bowl of food at every meal.

That's where the magic of Buddha Bowls steps in. Following a simple formula of **grain + green + protein**, these nourishing and tasty bowls are full of goodness that will restore you at the end of a long day or after a workout, and get you raring to go over lunch or in the morning.

But what *is* a Buddha Bowl?

Simply put, it is a bowl bursting with ingredients, so that it resembles the overstuffed belly of Buddha. Using a mix of ingredients, hot, cold and warm, Buddha Bowls aim to take the stress out of putting a meal together. Don't worry about having everything ready at the same time; instead, slowly assemble your bowl and mindfully enjoy the variety of temperatures, textures and flavours that eventually come together. Each of the recipes in this book contains the perfect balance to make a delicious meal for one – a meal that can be easily expanded to feed any number of people by simply multiplying the ingredients.

THE
BUDDHA
BOWLS
RITUAL

1. Take time to find your perfect bowl – one that fits perfectly into your cupped hands, or one whose appearance fills you with a feeling of joy, nourishment and gratitude.

2. Bed every bowl with an abundance of greens such as kale or spinach. These link us visually to nature, while filling the body with essential vitamins, minerals and fibre.

3. Then mix in raw and cooked veggies and enjoy the delicious mix of hot and cold, sweet and sour, crunchy and soft.

4. Add grains for an earthy texture and taste, and to fill you up, then protein to nourish your body and restore your muscles. Plant-based proteins are ideal for those following a vegan diet, while eggs and cheese have been included in various recipes for their superfood concentration of protein (and delicious-ness!).

5. Add your final flourish with a dressing or sauce: it can be anything from a simple drizzle of olive oil and balsamic vinegar to one of the tasty dressings or sauces in this book (see pages 21–27).

6. And finally, sit back, relax and take the time to enjoy every mouthful. Slowing down aids digestion and allows you to listen to the needs of your body as you eat.

GREENS AND RAW VEG

Kale

Spinach

Broccoli

Cucumber

Anything that grows!

Delicious raw vegetables, especially the green, leafy kind, are packed with vitamins, minerals, antioxidants and fibre that are often best absorbed when eaten raw. For extra nutrients, avoid peeling your vegetables and just give them a good rinse before eating – often a lot of the really good stuff is in the skin.

While the recipes in this book generally include green, leafy vegetables already, bear in mind that every flavour combination suggested can be supplemented with a big handful of spinach, kale or lettuce.

PROTEINS

Tofu	Eggs
Beans	Cheese
Lentils & pulses	Yoghurt
Quinoa	Labneh
Nuts	Kefir
Seeds	

Proteins are the essential building blocks for our muscles and general bodily repair. That's why it's important that each meal you eat is packed with protein, whether you are a vegetarian, vegan or meat-eater. All the bowls in this book contain a portion of protein, and the Recovery Bowls (see pages 80–95) pack an extra protein punch, perfect for recovering from the gym or a few too many late nights.

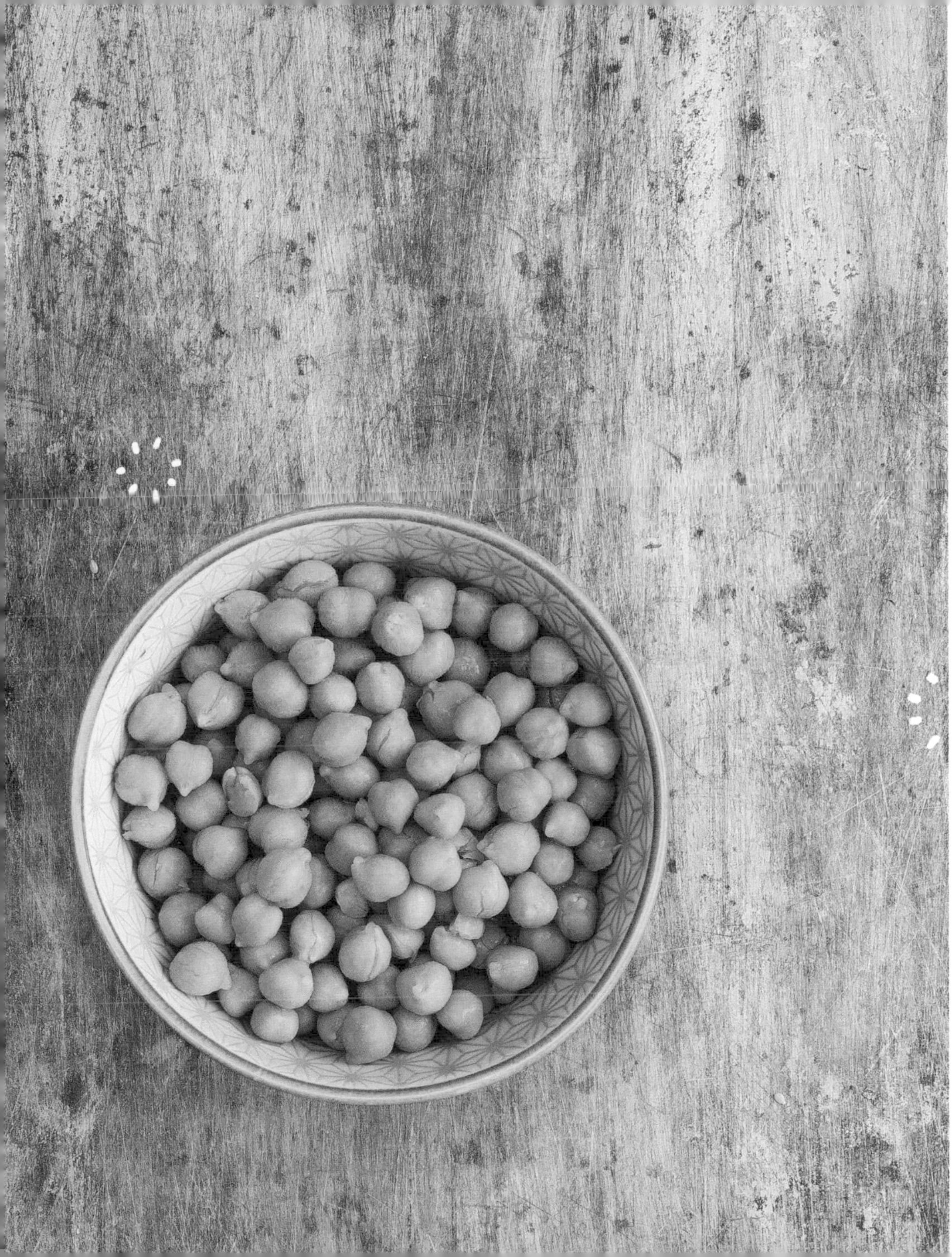

GRAINS

●

Wheat	Corn	Barley
Rye	Rice or Soba Noodles	Bran
Bulgur	Rice (gf)	Farina
Couscous	Oats (gf)	Kamut
Spelt	Quinoa (gf)	Polenta (gf)

Eating grains is essential not only for giving the body a healthy dose of carbohydrates that will keep it running all day, but also for providing fibre to keep digestion healthy. They release their energy slowly throughout the day, making them ideal components of lunch and breakfast as well as a filling dinner. The recipes here give the weight of grains when cooked – cook them as per packet instructions to get the desired weight. Although not all the grains listed here are used in this book, they make a great base for when you're starting to create your own bowls.

FRUIT & VEGGIES

Whether cooked or uncooked, fresh fruit and vegetables form an essential part of every diet. The recommended daily intake changes all the time, but one thing seems clear: we need to eat more fruit and veg! Embrace fruit and vegetables in Buddha Bowls where they add colour, flavour, texture and essential vitamins and minerals, whether cooked or uncooked.

DRESSINGS & SAUCES

If there is one thing that is sure to brighten up absolutely any bowl, it's a zingy and delicious sauce or dressing. The suggestions in this book can be made in advance, in bulk, and kept in the fridge for up to a week so they're ready to take out and drizzle over any bowl at a moment's notice.

Once you've got the sauces down, feel free to experiment with the bowls and pair your sauce with something unexpected. They're also a brilliant way to jazz up a dull salad, or you can spread them inside a sandwich to give it an extra hit of flavour.

FATS

●

Avocado

Coconut oil

Olive oil

Olives

Nuts

Seeds

Nut and seed oils

Far from making you pile on the pounds, healthy fats are essential for your body's development and continued health, and it is especially important to incorporate them into a meat- and fish-free diet.

17

STORE-CUPBOARD ESSENTIALS

Kitchen equipment:

A stick blender, food processor or NutriBullet
Small ovenproof dishes
A measuring jug
Scales
A small set of pans
A fork, for whisking
A sharp knife
A chopping board
A mandoline
A spiraliser or a grater
A beautiful bowl

For your store cupboard:

Olive oil, extra-virgin olive oil, vegetable oil
and sunflower oil
A selection of herbs and spices
Honey
Oats
Quinoa
Rice
Noodles

For your fridge:

A selection of seasonal fruit and vegetables
Leafy green vegetables such as spinach and kale
A stock of dressings and sauces (see pages 21–27)

VEGAN SWAPS

Yoghurt

In all cases, the yoghurt listed in the ingredients can be swapped for your preferred non-dairy alternative. Note that coconut and almond yoghurt will add a sweet, dessert-like taste, while oat or soya yoghurt will retain a more neutral and savoury flavour.

Cheese

Where cheeses such as halloumi or paneer are used, tofu will have a similar effect in terms of texture, appearance and protein content. Simply follow the recipe's cooking instructions using tofu in place of the hard cheese.

Eggs

Eggs can be substituted in most cases for another essential and healthy protein. For example, for Huevos Rancheros (see page 44), swap the eggs for kidney beans to give the dish just as much protein and to retain a Mexican feel.

Honey

Honey can always be swapped for maple or agave syrup to give the same sweet, sticky effect. Bee pollen can be left out wherever used.

Dressings & Sauces

A Buddha Bowl would be nothing without a swirl, splash or dollop of one of these delicious sauces or dressings. Whip them up in a jiffy and make extra so you can store them in the fridge and come back to them time and time again throughout the week.

AVOCADO LIME CREMA

2 avocados, peeled,
    stoned and diced
2 tbsp soured cream
    (or a non-dairy alternative)
Juice of 1 lime
A scrunch of sea salt

Equal parts zingy and creamy, this is a dream dressing that gives a Mexican flavour to any bowl – try it with Huevos Rancheros on page 44 or Piri Piri Tofu on page 100.

Blitz all the ingredients in a blender (a NutriBullet or similar works really well for sauces and dressings like this) until really smooth – this can take a couple of minutes. Store in the fridge until needed.

BANG BANG DRESSING

150g peanut butter
1 garlic clove, finely chopped
1 thumb-sized piece of fresh
    ginger, peeled and minced
Juice of 1 lime
1 tbsp rice vinegar
1 tbsp light soy sauce
1 tbsp maple syrup or honey
1 tbsp toasted sesame oil
50ml cold water

This explosively tasty sauce gives a real bang to any bowl it touches. Its distinctively Asian flavours team well with bowls such as Coconut Tofu on page 120.

Blitz all the ingredients in a food processor or blender until almost smooth and store in the fridge until needed.

These recipes make varying amounts depending on how saucy you like your bowl

BEETROOT YOGHURT

1 cooked beetroot (not pickled!), peeled and diced
300ml Greek yoghurt
Generous grind of black pepper

Simple yet startlingly effective, this bright pink dressing packs as much of a punch in its colour as it does in its flavour.

Blitz all the ingredients in a blender (a NutriBullet or similar works really well for sauces and dressings like this) until really smooth – this can take a couple of minutes. Store in the fridge until needed.

CHIPOTLE YOGHURT

220ml natural yoghurt
1 tbsp chipotle paste
Juice of 1 lime

A long-time favourite of Mexican restaurants worldwide, this delicious dip is devilishly easy to make.

Mix all the ingredients together in a bowl until just rippled and keep in the fridge until needed.

DIJON DRESSING

1 tsp Dijon mustard
3 tbsp white wine vinegar
2 tbsp extra-virgin olive oil
Sea salt and black pepper
A pinch of sugar

An absolute classic. It's worth investing in some high-quality Dijon mustard to really make this sauce sing. Team it with crunchy, fresh greens like those in Red Onion and Broccoli on page 79.

Mix all the ingredients together in a bowl, then pour into a jug and keep in the fridge until needed.

6

POMEGRANATE DRESSING

100ml pomegranate
  molasses
50ml date syrup
2 tbsp extra-virgin
  olive oil

This one is mad-fruity and juicy, and great with Middle Eastern flavours like chopped salads and falafel.

Pour all the ingredients into a bottle, seal and shake together well until combined. Store in the fridge until needed.

SMOKY CARROT SAUCE

500g carrots, peeled and
  cut into chunks
Sea salt
50ml olive oil, plus extra
  for cooking
1 tsp smoked paprika
50ml extra-virgin olive oil
50ml cold water
25ml rice vinegar
Juice of 1 lemon

Think of this as carrot hummus – it has the same texture and a similarly smoky and addictive flavour.

Preheat your oven to 180°C (fan). While it's heating, parboil your carrots in boiling water for 10 minutes, then drain.

Lay the carrots out in a baking tray and lightly coat them with a drizzle of olive oil and a scrunch of sea salt. Roast in the oven for 50 minutes, turning occasionally. You're looking for them to colour up around the edges. During the last 20 minutes of cooking, sprinkle them with the paprika.

Remove the carrots from the oven and blitz in a food processor with all the other ingredients until smooth. This will take a few minutes and you'll be left with a thick sauce. Store in the fridge until needed.

TAHINI GOAT'S YOGHURT

120ml goat's yoghurt
4 tsp tahini
4 tsp runny honey
1 tsp sriracha
1 tsp lemon juice

A classic case of less is more; this sauce is sweet, sticky and ever so moreish.

Mix all the ingredients together in a bowl and keep in the fridge until needed.

Morning Bowls

Get yourself in the mood for whatever the day has in store
with these appetising and filling Morning Bowls. Each one
is full of the protein, nutrients and energy you need for
the day ahead, not to mention being so packed with flavour
you'll (almost) dance right out of bed to eat them.

CHIA PUDDING

●

This creamy and sweet breakfast pudding, bursting with fruits and nutty almond milk, tastes so good it feels like something you shouldn't be allowed to eat for breakfast.

50g white chia seeds, plus
    extra for sprinkling
200ml almond milk
½ ripe mango
½ ripe papaya
100ml Greek yoghurt
½ tsp matcha powder
2 tbsp runny honey
A sprinkle of bee pollen
A few leaves of fresh mint
A small handful of blueberries
    and raspberries

Mix the chia and almond milk together in a bowl and wait until the seeds start to swell – around 10 minutes. While you're waiting, use a food processor to blitz the mango and papaya flesh into a smooth purée.

In a separate bowl, mix the yoghurt and matcha powder together with 1 tablespoon of the honey. Place the chia mixture in a bowl with the fruit purée and matcha yoghurt, top with a sprinkle of chia seeds, bee pollen (if you wish) and mint, the remaining honey and the berries.

TROPICAL OVERNIGHT OATS

•

Overnight oats are an Instagram favourite that can be made the night before for an easy grab-and-go breakfast. Here they meet the tropical flavours of mango, nectarines and coconut to add some sunshine to your morning routine.

155ml almond milk
55g oats
A handful of diced mango
1 ripe nectarine, sliced
2 tbsp coconut yoghurt
2 tbsp toasted crushed
  hazelnuts

If you're toasting your own hazelnuts, do this ahead of time.

The night before you want to eat, mix the almond milk and oats together in a bowl, cover and place in the fridge. The next morning, add to the bowl the mango and nectarine, coconut yoghurt and crushed hazelnuts.

ENGLISH ORCHARD OVERNIGHT OATS

●

Crunchy apple crisps add texture to this creamy overnight oat breakfast that draws on the flavours of an English orchard in summer.

2 apples, cored
155ml almond milk
55g oats
A handful of diced fresh
    strawberries
A handful of fresh raspberries
2 tbsp soya yoghurt

The night before you want to eat, preheat your oven to 150°C (fan).

Slice the apples very thinly (about 2mm thick) – using a mandoline is ideal. Lay the apple slices out on a baking tray lined with baking parchment, making sure they don't overlap. Bake in the oven for 12–18 minutes, turning them every 6 minutes, until they're lightly golden – keep an eye on them, as they burn easily. Remove from the oven and place on a board to cool. Store in a Tupperware box.

Mix the almond milk and oats together in a bowl, then cover and place in the fridge overnight.

The next morning, add to the bowl the strawberries and raspberries, soya yoghurt and top with the apple crisps.

NUT BUTTER OATS

●

**These delicious and protein-rich oats are an amazing way
to start your day – not only are they tasty, but they will also
slowly release energy throughout the day.**

155ml soya milk
55g oats
2 tbsp almond butter, or which-
    ever nut butter you prefer
2 fresh strawberries, sliced
A handful of dried cranberries
A handful of fresh blueberries
1 tsp cacao nibs
A drizzle of runny honey

The night before you want to eat, mix the soya milk and
oats together in a bowl, cover and place in the fridge.
The next morning, add to the bowl the nut butter, berries,
cacao and runny honey.

∿ RHUBARB RIPPLE ∿

●

200g rhubarb, diced
1 thumb-sized piece of fresh
  ginger, peeled and grated
4 tbsp light agave syrup
30ml cold water
150ml Greek yoghurt

Like the much-loved seaside favourite, the raspberry ripple, this rhubarb cousin is bursting with sweet and sour flavour and is a really punchy way to start your day.

Place the rhubarb, ginger, agave and cold water in a pan over a medium heat. When the rhubarb softens and starts to shred after 8-12 minutes, taste and adjust the sweetness by adding more agave as needed. Take off the heat and leave to cool. Swirl in a bowl briefly with the Greek yoghurt to create the ripple effect.

∿ FRUIT SMOOTHIE BOWL ∿

●

100ml coconut yoghurt
½ ripe mango
1 just-ripe banana
6 fresh strawberries
35g Granola (optional,
  see recipe on page 38)
2 tbsp coconut flakes
  (optional)

This is a fruit smoothie that you can eat! All the goodness is blitzed in a blender, and if you really want to have it on the go then just skip the granola and flaked coconut and take it with you as you head out the door.

Blitz the coconut yoghurt in a blender or food processor with the mango, banana and strawberries. Pour into a bowl and scatter with the granola and coconut flakes, if you like.

WATERMELON AND RICE PUDDING

•

The creaminess of this rice pudding is offset by the refreshing watermelon, making it the dream summer breakfast. This can be made in advance as it has a long cooking time.

50g pudding rice
400ml full-fat cow's milk
　or almond milk
1 vanilla pod, seeds
　scraped out
100ml light agave syrup
A pinch of sea salt
200g diced watermelon
A handful of dried cranberries
2 tbsp coconut or goat's
　yoghurt
A sprinkle of bee pollen

The night before you want to eat, preheat your oven to 150°C (fan). In an ovenproof dish combine the rice, milk, vanilla (the pod and the seeds), agave and salt, mix together and bake, uncovered, for 2–2½ hours, stirring a couple of times. Keep an eye on it and cover it with foil if it begins to brown too quickly. Remove from the oven and leave to cool, then store in the fridge.

In the morning, spoon the rice pudding into a bowl (remove the vanilla pod as you do so) and top with the watermelon and cranberries, then finish with the yoghurt and a sprinkling of bee pollen (if you wish).

GRANOLA

•

The original hippie food! Nothing sets you up for the day better than a bowl of well-balanced granola. This will store well in an airtight jar.

120ml almond milk
2 tbsp coconut yoghurt
Fresh fruit of your choice, such as plums, diced, and blueberries

For the granola:
1 tsp vanilla extract
125ml agave syrup
2 tbsp runny honey
2 tbsp vegetable oil
300g oats
50g sunflower seeds
50g pumpkin seeds
Sea salt
50g coconut flakes
100g almond flakes
100g dried berries

Preheat your oven to 150°C (fan).

First, make the granola. In a large bowl, mix together the vanilla, agave, honey and oil. Add the oats, sunflower and pumpkin seeds and a small scrunch of salt.

Lay out the granola evenly across two baking trays lined with baking parchment and place in the oven for 12 minutes, then add the coconut and almond flakes and the dried berries, stir the mix and return to the oven for another 12 minutes until the granola is lightly toasted. Remove from the oven and scoop the granola out onto a sheet of baking parchment to cool and crisp up.

Pile a portion of the granola into a bowl and top with the almond milk, the coconut yoghurt, the diced fruit and an extra scattering of the granola.

BEETROOT AND QUINOA PORRIDGE

●

'Beetroot with porridge?!' I hear you scream. Open your mind to the possibility of the deliciously sweet side of beetroot – perfect when teamed with quinoa and zingy lemon.

40g quinoa
150ml soy or almond milk
¼ tsp vanilla extract
2 tbsp runny honey
A small pinch of sea salt
1 kiwi fruit, peeled and sliced
A small handful of fresh
   blueberries
A small handful of toasted
   hazelnuts, roughly chopped
1 tsp shredded coconut
Beetroot Yoghurt (see recipe
   on page 25)

If you're toasting your own hazelnuts, do this ahead of time.

Rinse the quinoa and put it in a pan with the milk, vanilla, honey and salt. Bring to the boil, then reduce the heat to its lowest setting and allow the porridge to cook for about 15 minutes, stirring frequently.

Serve the hot quinoa porridge with the Beetroot Yoghurt and top with the kiwi fruit, blueberries, hazelnuts and coconut.

PEA PESTO AND POACHED EGG

●

Enjoy the guilty pleasure of having pesto for breakfast in this deliciously balanced bowl. It works perfectly for a satisfying brunch as well.

100g cooked brown rice, warm
  or cold
White wine vinegar
1 egg
1 avocado, peeled, stoned
  and sliced

*For the pesto:**
A large bunch of fresh coriander
35g cashews, dry toasted in
  a pan
1 garlic clove, peeled
100ml light olive oil
50ml extra-virgin olive oil
Juice of 1 lemon
Sea salt and black pepper
100g frozen petits pois, thawed

*This makes more than is needed for the recipe and will keep, if covered in oil, for 7 days in the fridge

First, make the pea pesto. Place the coriander, cashews, garlic, olive oils, lemon juice and a scrunch of salt and a grind of black pepper in a food processor and blitz until a coarse paste forms. Add the thawed peas and blend again – scraping the sides down in the processor so all the ingredients are caught – until a coarse, medium-thick paste forms. Taste for seasoning and add more salt if needed.

Stir 4 tablespoons of the pea pesto through the cooked brown rice and pile it into a bowl.

Heat a pan of water and add a scrunch of salt and a splash of white wine vinegar. When it's at a rolling boil crack the egg into the water and cook for 2 minutes for a soft-poached egg, then remove with a slotted spoon and place on kitchen paper to drain. Add the egg to the bowl on top of the rice, alongside the avocado.

FROZEN BERRY YOGHURT

●

This is as close as you can come to having ice cream for breakfast, and it is absolutely full of good-for-you vitamins and fats.

50g white chia seeds
200ml almond milk
160ml Greek yoghurt
50g frozen raspberries
  and blackberries
60ml agave syrup,
  plus extra for drizzling
A handful of fresh
  strawberries, sliced
A handful of toasted
  crushed hazelnuts, skinned

If you're toasting your own hazelnuts, do this ahead of time.

Mix the chia and almond milk together in a bowl and wait until the seeds start to swell – around 10 minutes. While you're waiting, use a food processor to blitz together the yoghurt, frozen raspberries and blackberries and agave until creamy – about 5 minutes.

When the chia mixture is ready, put it into a bowl with the frozen yoghurt and top with the strawberries, crushed hazelnuts and a drizzle of agave.

HUEVOS RANCHEROS

●

All hail the queen of the brunch table: huevos rancheros!
This balanced Buddha-Bowls version of this well-loved Mexican
egg dish has all the flavour and plenty of sustenance to get
you ready to take on the day.

200g sweet potato, diced
Olive oil
1 red pepper, diced
1 green pepper, diced
½ tsp smoked paprika
Sea salt
White wine vinegar
1 egg
100g cooked brown rice
  (still warm)
Avocado Lime Crema
  (see recipe on page 22)
A handful of fresh coriander
  leaves
1 tsp toasted sesame seeds
Chilli sauce such as sriracha,
  to serve

Preheat your oven to 190°C (fan).

Boil the sweet potato for 7 minutes, then allow it to cool.

Lightly oil a roasting dish and add the diced sweet potatoes to one half of the pan and the peppers to the other. Lightly drizzle them with olive oil and sprinkle the potatoes with smoked paprika and sea salt. Bake for 35 minutes, stirring occasionally.

Towards the end of cooking, heat a pan of water and add a pinch of sea salt and a splash of white wine vinegar. When it's at a rolling boil crack the egg into the water and cook for 2 minutes for a soft-poached egg, then remove with a slotted spoon and place on kitchen paper to drain.

Remove the peppers and potato from the oven. Set the peppers aside and mix the brown rice and sweet potato together.

Pile the potato and rice into a bowl with the roasted peppers and top with the poached egg, Avocado Lime Crema, coriander and sesame seeds. Serve with the chilli sauce on the side.

Lunch
Bowls

All of these delicious lunch bowls can be easily assembled from leftovers or made the night before to keep your morning clear and easy. Simply pack them up in a Tupperware container and take with you to keep you fuelled all day. If you have a little more time or are having lunch at home, assemble them from scratch in your favourite bowl and enjoy a quiet moment of ritual in the middle of a hectic day.

TOMATO AND BASIL SILKEN TOFU

•

This indulgent and delicious dish is full of Italian flavours and makes a cosy dish for one. The silken tofu adds an unexpected texture and a welcome kick of plant-based protein.

Olive oil
350g firm silken tofu
1 small garlic clove, minced
50g sundried tomatoes,
    finely chopped
3 tbsp chopped tomatoes
    or passata
Juice of ½ lemon, plus extra
    for squeezing
200g cooked bulgur wheat,
    warm or cold
Extra-virgin olive oil
Sea salt and black pepper
1 courgette, spiralised
2 tbsp goat's yoghurt
1 tsp toasted sesame seeds
A handful of fresh basil leaves

Preheat your oven to 190°C (fan).

Lightly oil a roasting dish and carefully place the firm silken tofu in it. Mix the garlic and sundried tomatoes with the chopped tomatoes or passata and spoon over the tofu. Bake in the oven for 30 minutes.

While that's cooking, add the lemon juice to the bulgur wheat with a glug of extra-virgin olive oil, and season to taste with sea salt and black pepper.

Place the bulgur wheat at the bottom of a bowl and top with the freshly spiralised courgette, giving it a squeeze of lemon. Top with the hot silken tofu, being careful when you get it out of the dish, as it's very soft. Spoon over the goat's yoghurt and sesame seeds, adding a squeeze of lemon, and finish with the fresh basil.

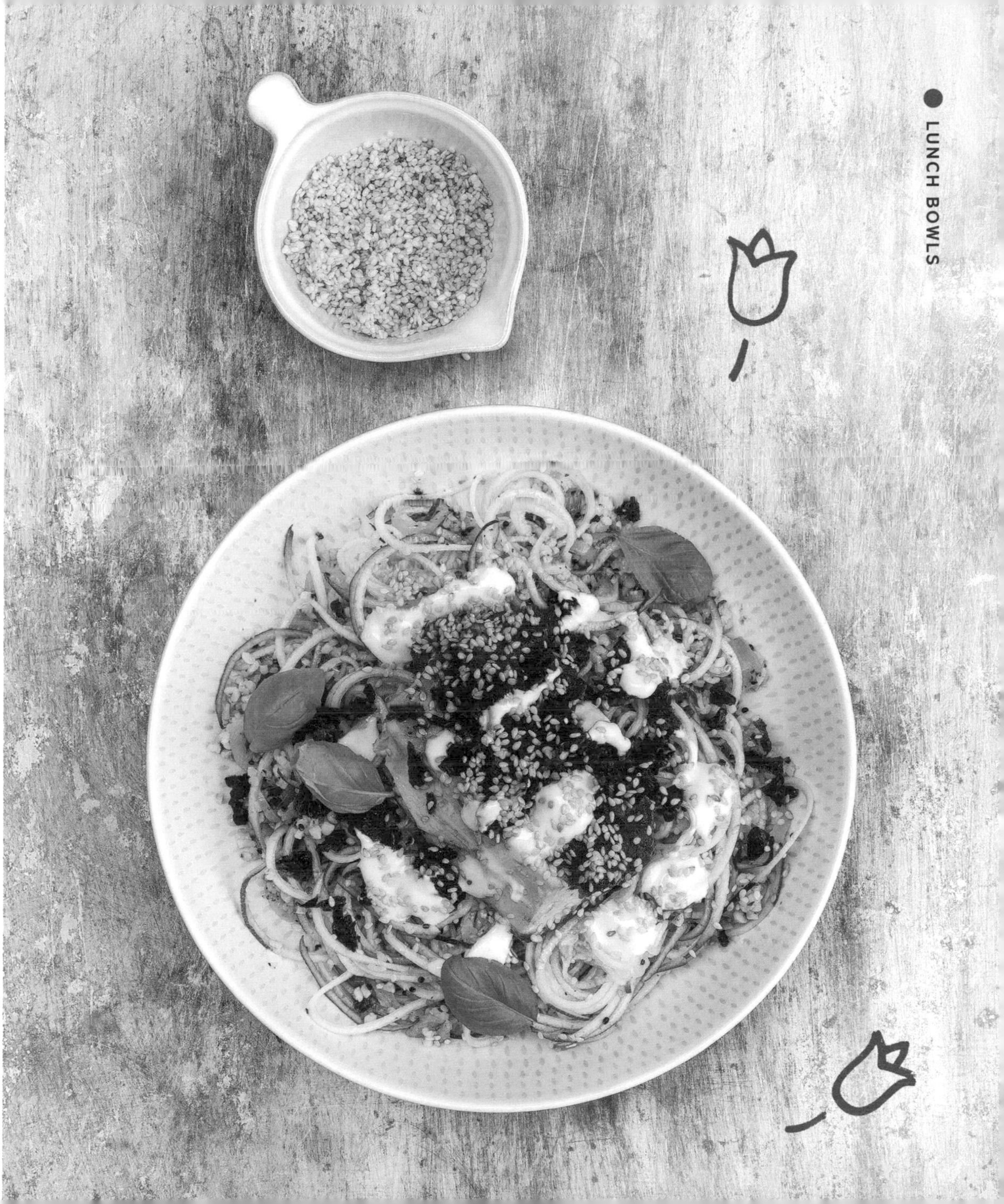

PEA AND FETA OMELETTE

●

**Omelettes are an easy and quick way to get some protein into
your lunch – this version contains quinoa for an extra hit.**

100g feta, crumbled
100g frozen petits pois, thawed
2 eggs, lightly beaten and
  seasoned with salt
Light olive oil
200g cooked mixed white
  and black quinoa, served
  warm
Sea salt and black pepper
Chipotle Yoghurt (see recipe
  on page 25)
A large handful of rocket
1 tbsp toasted sesame seeds

Mix the feta and thawed peas into the beaten egg. Heat a little light olive oil in a frying pan over a medium heat, add the egg mixture and let it cook (without stirring) for a couple of minutes, then carefully flip the whole thing over and turn off the heat; the egg will cook through in the residual heat.

Pile the cooked quinoa into a bowl and turn the omelette out on top of it. Finish with a dollop of the Chipotle Yoghurt and the rocket and sesame seeds. Season to taste.

SPICY GLASS NOODLES

●

**Glass noodles make this a beautiful bowl to look at – it's one
to linger over when lunchtime allows.**

Olive oil
1 red pepper, diced
1 small red onion, diced
2 handfuls of chestnut
   mushrooms, brushed of any
   dirt (but not washed), diced
2 handfuls of kale
1 thumb-sized piece of fresh
   ginger, peeled and grated
1 small garlic clove,
   finely chopped
Sea salt and black pepper
2 tbsp runny honey
1 tbsp tahini
½ tsp sriracha
Juice of ½ lime
2 x 40g packs of glass noodles,
   soaked in cold water and
   cooked then cooled
1 large carrot, spiralised
1 tsp black sesame seeds
A handful of fresh coriander
   leaves

Preheat your oven to 180°C (fan) and lightly oil a baking tray.

Mix together the red pepper, red onion and chestnut mushrooms
and drizzle with olive oil. Put them in the baking tray and bake for
20 minutes, turning the vegetables once. Add the kale to the baking
tray with a little more oil, the ginger and garlic, season to taste with
salt and pepper and bake for another 10 minutes.

While that's cooking, combine the honey, tahini, sriracha, ginger,
garlic and lime etc. then mix through the drained glass noodles.
Pile the noodles into a bowl and top with the roasted veggies,
tossing together. Finish with the spiralised carrot, sesame seeds,
lime juice and fresh coriander.

WATERMELON AND HALLOUMI

●

**Zingy and fresh, this is the ideal lunch bowl, filling you up but
leaving your stomach feeling light and nourished with the summer
flavours of mint and watermelon.**

A small handful of fresh mint
  leaves, shredded
Juice of ½ lime
Sea salt and black pepper
200g cooked couscous, cooled
125g halloumi, cut into strips
2 tbsp runny honey
200g diced watermelon
A handful of chopped
  cucumber
A handful of shelled
  pistachios
A wedge of lime, to serve

Preheat your frying pan with no oil on a medium-high heat.
While it's heating, combine the mint, lime juice and seasoning
(to taste) to the couscous and season to taste. Set aside.

In the frying pan, sear the halloumi strips on both sides until
golden and then remove from the heat. Place the halloumi with
the minted couscous in a bowl, drizzle with honey and serve with
the watermelon, cucumber, pistachios and a wedge of lime.

BLACK QUINOA
AND HALLOUMI

•

**Black quinoa adds an unexpectedly rich colour to this
bowl, which is then offset by the bright colours of the squash,
carrot and avocado. A pretty lunchtime bowl with a mix of
textures and flavours.**

Olive oil
150g butternut squash,
   diced
Sea salt
250g block halloumi, diced
200g cooked black quinoa,
   still warm
A handful of finely shredded
   red cabbage
A handful of grated carrot
Pomegranate Dressing
   (see recipe on page 26)
½ avocado, peeled, stoned
   and finely sliced

Preheat your oven to 180°C (fan) and lightly oil a baking tray.

Add the diced squash, lightly drizzle with olive oil and season with
a little sea salt. Bake for 30 minutes, turning the squash twice.
During the last 15 minutes of cooking, add the diced halloumi.

Into a bowl, pile the cooked quinoa, cabbage and carrot, and
dress with 3 tablespoons of the Pomegranate Dressing. Add
the avocado slices and finish with the hot squash and halloumi,
tossing everything together.

SMOKY ALMONDS
AND SWEET POTATO

●

The smoky almonds are the secret to this lunch bowl, which is packed with classic Buddha-Bowl flavours: sweet potato and avocado.

Olive oil
1 sweet potato, peeled and cut into large chunks
1 tsp sea salt, plus extra for seasoning
100g almonds, skin on
1 tbsp groundnut oil
1 heaped tsp smoked paprika
3 tbsp Greek yoghurt
¼ cucumber, peeled, deseeded and finely chopped
A squeeze of lemon
1 avocado, peeled, stoned and roughly chopped
100g flaxseed crackers, crumbled
1 red chilli, finely chopped

Preheat your oven to 190°C (fan).

Lightly oil a baking tray and add the sweet potato chunks, drizzling with olive oil and seasoning with salt. Bake for 25 minutes.

Put the almonds and groundnut oil in a mixing bowl and toss to coat, then lay them out in a single layer on a baking tray and bake for 10 minutes, shaking once. Remove from the oven and sprinkle with the smoked paprika and 1 teaspoon of sea salt, and mix together thoroughly.

In a separate small bowl mix together the Greek yoghurt, cucumber and lemon juice and season with salt.

Pile the hot sweet potato into a bowl, top with the avocado chunks, smoky almonds and Greek yoghurt mixture, and finish with the flaxseed crackers and chopped chilli.

Keep any leftover almonds in an airtight container so they don't lose their crunch.

BEETROOT FALAFEL

For the falafel:
125g raw beetroot, peeled and
    coarsely grated
200g tinned chickpeas,
    drained and rinsed
½ onion, diced
1 garlic clove, peeled
1 tsp ground coriander
1 tsp ground cumin
½ tsp salt
75g wholemeal breadcrumbs
½ beaten egg
A small handful of fresh
    coriander, stalks included

100g cooked giant
    couscous, cooled
100g cauliflower 'rice'
50g cooked black rice or millet,
    warm or cold
100g raw broccoli stems,
    peeled and diced
A pinch of chopped fresh
    parsley
Juice of 1 lime
Extra-virgin olive oil
Sea salt and black pepper
A handful of sprouting seeds
A handful of fresh watercress
Chipotle Yoghurt (see recipe
    on page 25)
1 tsp sunflower seeds
A wedge of lime, to serve

Falafel comes in many forms, but this beetroot incarnation is packed full of flavour and texture, and is both decadent and good for you. To make meals easier throughout the week, make twice as many falafels and store them in the fridge to spice up salads and sandwiches at a moment's notice!

Preheat your oven to 190°C (fan).

In a food processor combine all the falafel ingredients apart from about one-third of the raw grated beetroot and a scattering of chickpeas. Blitz until just smooth and transfer to a mixing bowl. Add the remaining beetroot and mix to combine. Form into falafel balls and bake on a lined baking sheet in the oven for 25 minutes, turning once during cooking.

While they are cooking, combine the couscous, cauliflower 'rice', black rice or millet, broccoli stems and parsley in a bowl with half the lime juice and a glug of extra-virgin olive oil, then season with salt and pepper to taste.

Pile the grains in a bowl with the sprouting seeds and top with the hot falafel. Finish with the watercress, a drizzle of the remaining lime juice over the falafel, a drizzle of the Chipotle Yoghurt, the sunflower seeds and a wedge of lime.

ROASTED CAULIFLOWER AND BEETROOT YOGHURT

●

Roasted cauliflower is a hearty lunchtime treat, and beetroot yoghurt adds a shock of pink that will pep you up for the afternoon ahead.

Olive oil
1 small cauliflower head, cut into florets
Sea salt and black pepper
½ red pepper, finely diced
½ orange pepper, finely diced
A handful of fresh basil leaves, finely chopped
¼ cucumber, deseeded and finely diced
4 juicy tomatoes, deseeded and finely diced
2 handfuls of fresh spinach, finely chopped
¼ small red onion, finely diced
½ small garlic clove, finely chopped
Juice of 1 lemon
Extra-virgin olive oil (the same volume as the lemon juice)
200g cooked white quinoa, cooled
Beetroot Yoghurt (see recipe on page 25)
A handful of pumpkin and sesame seeds

Preheat your oven to 190°C (fan).

Lightly oil a baking tray and add the cauliflower florets, drizzle in olive oil and season with salt. Bake in the oven for 40 minutes, turning a couple of times during cooking so the cauliflower starts to really colour up – that's when it's at its tastiest!

While that's cooking, toss together in a bowl the peppers, basil, cucumber, tomatoes, spinach, red onion, garlic, lemon juice and extra-virgin olive oil, and season with salt and pepper.

Pile the quinoa into a bowl and add the chopped salad. Top with the roasted cauliflower and dress with a dollop of the Beetroot Yoghurt, scattering the seeds over the top.

CHARRED CORN AND SPICED CHICKPEAS

●

A light and summery bowl, this is perfect for capturing that BBQ feeling all year round. Best enjoyed on a sunny afternoon, taking stock of the day in the garden, possibly with a beer...

1 x 400g tin chickpeas, drained and rinsed
2 tbsp ras-el-hanout spice blend
1 corn cob, lightly oiled
A handful of fresh spinach, finely chopped
150g cooked farro, still warm
Sea salt and black pepper
½ avocado, peeled, stoned and thinly sliced
Chipotle Yoghurt (see recipe on page 25)
A squeeze of lemon
A pinch of chilli flakes (optional)
Extra leaves, to serve, such as watercress, rocket or more spinach (optional)

Preheat your oven to 190°C (fan).

Coat your chickpeas in the spice mixture and spread them out on a baking tray. Bake for 20–30 minutes until they've really coloured up, shaking the tray occasionally to make sure they colour evenly all over.

While they're cooking, preheat your griddle for 5 minutes on a high heat. Lightly oil the corn cob and place on the griddle, turning the cob occasionally for 6–8 minutes until it's lightly charred. Remove from the heat and leave until cool enough to be handled.

Mix the spinach through the cooked farro, season with salt and pepper and set aside.

Remove the chickpeas from the oven and season straight away with salt. Cut the corn kernels off the cob and add to a bowl with the hot chickpeas, spinach and farro, the sliced avocado and a dollop of the Chipotle Yoghurt. Squeeze over some lemon and if you like it hot add a pinch of chilli flakes. Serve with some extra leaves if you like.

FETA, KALETTES AND CRISPY LINSEEDS

●

Crispy roasted linseeds are the secret to this light and flavoursome bowl, while the quintessential marriage of beetroot and quinoa reaches new heights with a heart-healthy kick of lemon and garlic.

60 Kalettes
Olive oil
1 garlic clove, finely chopped
Sea salt and black pepper
1 raw beetroot, juiced,
   or 100ml shop-bought
   beetroot juice
1 cooked beetroot (not
   pickled!), peeled and diced
200g cooked quinoa, warm
   or cold
Juice of ½ lemon
1 carrot, grated
1 courgette, grated
100g feta, crumbled
Smoky Carrot Sauce
   (see recipe on page 27)
Store-bought pesto

For the soy-roasted linseeds: *
2 tbsp groundnut or
   sunflower oil
1 tbsp light soy sauce
200g golden linseeds

Preheat your oven to 160°C (fan).

First, make the soy-roasted linseeds. Mix the oil and soy sauce together and pour over the linseeds in a bowl, stirring thoroughly to coat. Spread out on a baking tray and bake for 20 minutes, stirring the seeds with a fork halfway through the cooking time. Remove from the oven and set aside to cool – this delicious snack keeps well in an airtight jar and goes well on bowls of all kinds.

Increase the oven temperature to 190°C (fan).

Rinse and dry the Kalettes and place on a lightly oiled baking sheet. Drizzle with a little olive oil, add the garlic, season with salt and pepper and bake for 10 minutes.

While the Kalettes are baking, take the beetroot juice and diced beetroot and mix them through the cooked quinoa in a bowl. Add the lemon juice and a scrunch of sea salt and set aside.

Place the beetroot quinoa, grated carrot and courgette in a bowl and pile on the hot Kalettes and crumbled feta. Finish with the Smoky Carrot Sauce or a store-bought pesto, and a generous sprinkling of the soy-roasted linseeds.

*This makes more than the recipe needs, but they keep well in an airtight container

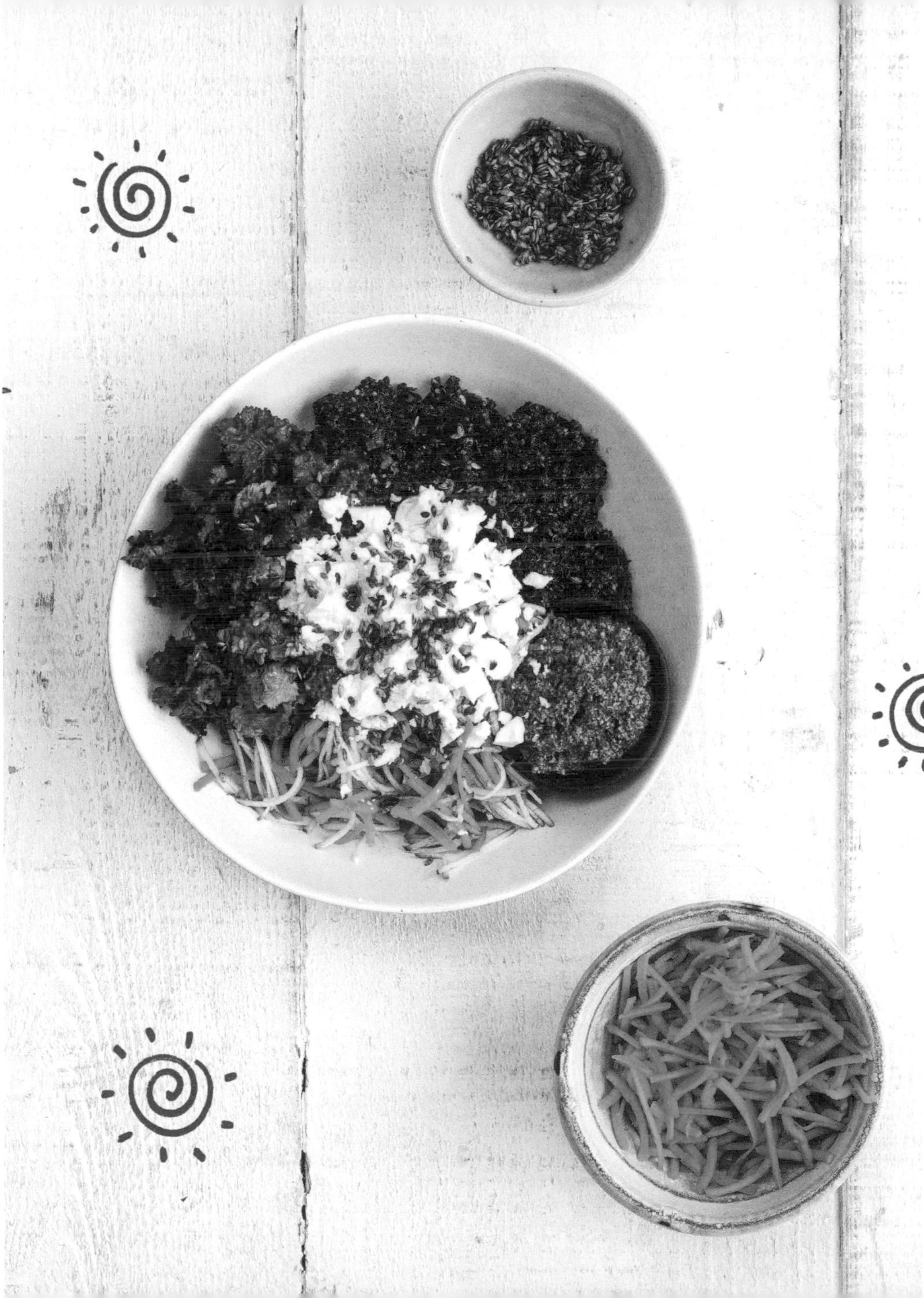

Evening Bowls

At the end of a long day, what could be better than tucking into a nourishing and balanced bowl of goodness? From hearty salads to warm meals, these bowls will leave you satisfied without confining you to the kitchen all evening.

BAKED FETA
WITH PISTACHIO PESTO

•

Let feta take centre stage in this delicious evening bowl that is ideal for when the evenings start to get a little warmer and you need something more inspiring than your go-to Greek salad.

Light olive oil
½ red pepper, cut into
  large chunks
½ yellow pepper,
  cut into large chunks
200g block feta, crumbled
  or sliced
Sea salt and black pepper
2 tbsp pistachio pesto
200g cooked green lentils,
  warm or cold
1 small courgette, finely grated
Juice of 1 lemon
A pinch of chopped fresh
  basil leaves
A pinch of toasted sesame
  seeds
1 tbsp shelled pistachios
Extra-virgin olive oil

Preheat your oven to 180°C (fan).

Lightly oil a baking tray and add the chopped peppers, tossing to lightly coat them in the oil. Bake in the oven for 40 minutes until softened and starting to char around the edges, then remove from the oven and set aside.

Take a few strips of the peppers and place in a lightly oiled baking dish. Top with the feta, season with black pepper and return to the oven. Bake for 20–30 minutes, until the feta is lightly browning and softened.

Mix the pistachio pesto through the green lentils and season with salt and pepper to taste.

Remove the feta from the oven and set aside. Pile the green lentils, roasted peppers and grated courgette into a bowl. Give it all a big squeeze of lemon and then place the feta on top, finishing with the chopped basil, sesame seeds and pistachios and a glug of your favourite extra-virgin olive oil.

ROAST MUSHROOMS AND FENNEL

●

Fennel is incredibly good for your gut, and also gives this recipe of earthy mushrooms a refreshing aniseed kick.

Olive oil
200g chestnut mushrooms, brushed of any dirt (but not washed)
1 fennel bulb, quartered
A handful of asparagus, stems trimmed
Dijon Dressing (see recipe on page 26)
A handful of fresh parsley leaves, finely chopped
Juice of ½ lemon
200g puy lentils, still warm
Sea salt
A handful of toasted skinned hazelnuts, roughly chopped

Preheat your oven to 190°C (fan).

Lightly oil a baking tray and put the mushrooms and fennel quarters on it. Bake in the oven for 30 minutes, turning the mushrooms and fennel twice.

During the last 10 minutes of cooking, preheat your griddle for 5 minutes over a high heat. Place the asparagus on the griddle and cook, turning the spears regularly, for about 5 minutes, until they're lightly charred (keep an eye on the tips!).

Remove from the heat and take the mushrooms and fennel out of the oven to make sure they don't burn. Lightly brush the mushrooms, asparagus and fennel with the Dijon Dressing.

Mix the parsley and lemon juice through the lentils and pile them into a bowl and add the vegetables, scattering with the toasted hazelnuts. Season to taste.

BEETROOT HUMMUS AND BLACK BEANS

●

Black beans are such a treat when teamed with beetroot hummus. Packed with protein, this is a bowl to pep you up at the end of a long, long day. Use the crackers as you would nachos, to scoop up the good stuff.

100g cooked black beans, still warm

100g cooked bulgur wheat, still warm

1 courgette, finely grated

A large handful of flaxseed crackers or corn nachos

For the sriracha dressing:
½ tsp sriracha
2 tsp runny honey
Juice of 1 lime
A dash of light soy sauce

For the beetroot hummus:
1 x 400g tin chickpeas, drained and rinsed
1 cooked beetroot (not pickled!), peeled and diced
2 tbsp tahini
2 garlic cloves, peeled
Juice of 1 lemon
Sea salt and black pepper
100ml extra-virgin olive oil

First, make the sriracha dressing. Mix together the sriracha, honey, lime juice and soy sauce in a bowl, and set aside.

Next, make the beetroot hummus. Place the chickpeas, beetroot, tahini, garlic, half the lemon juice and a generous scrunch of salt in a food processor and blitz until smooth. Add the extra-virgin olive oil and blitz again, then transfer to a bowl.

Mix the black beans and bulgur wheat together with the courgette and pile into a bowl. Dress with the remaining lemon juice and season with salt and pepper. Drizzle with the sriracha dressing and add the beetroot hummus to the bowl with the flaxseed crackers, or corn nachos as an alternative.

SUPER-NUTTY SESAME TOFU

●

**With a deep, nutty flavour and texture, the plant-based protein
in this dish is coming at you from all angles: tofu, groundnut oil,
sesame seeds, bulgur wheat and pumpkin seeds galore.**

50ml soy sauce
20ml groundnut oil
250g firm tofu, drained,
   pressed and diced*
1 tsp toasted sesame seeds
1 tbsp toasted sesame oil
A handful of grated carrot
A handful of grated red cabbage
Juice of 1 lime
200g cooked bulgur wheat,
   cooled
A handful of fresh spinach
Smoky Carrot Sauce
   (see recipe on page 27)

*For the soy-roasted pumpkin
   seeds:***
2 tbsp groundnut or
   sunflower oil
1 tbsp light soy sauce
200g pumpkin seeds

Mix the soy sauce and groundnut oil together and toss the tofu in it,
turning to coat, and leave to stand for at least 1 hour.

Next, make the soy-roasted seeds. Preheat your oven to 200°C
(fan). Mix the oil and soy together and pour over the seeds, stirring
thoroughly to coat. Spread over a lined baking sheet and bake for
20 minutes, stirring with a fork halfway through cooking. Remove and
set aside to cool – these delicious snacks go well on bowls of all kinds.

Lightly oil a baking sheet and lay out the tofu, then bake for 20–30
minutes until it starts to really colour up. About 5–10 minutes before
the end of cooking, add the sesame seeds and, on removing the tofu
from the oven, drizzle with the sesame oil and turn to coat.

Mix together the carrot and cabbage with the lime juice and pile
into a bowl with the bulgur wheat, 1 tablespoon of the pumpkin
seeds, spinach and tofu, finishing with the Smoky Carrot Sauce.

*To press tofu,
simply press it
between two plates,
with a weight on top,
to remove excess
water.

** This makes more than the recipe needs, but they keep well in an airtight container

SOBA NOODLES AND SEAWEED
WITH SHIITAKE 'BACON'

●

Seaweed gives a rich yet subtle umami undercurrent to this bowl.

3 tsp groundnut or
   vegetable oil
6 tsp tamari or soy sauce
2 tsp maple syrup
15 shiitake mushrooms,
   thinly sliced
A pinch of garlic powder
¼ tsp smoked paprika
Sea salt and black pepper
200ml vegetable stock
1 thumb-sized piece of fresh
   ginger, peeled and grated
1 tsp ground kelp or laver
   seaweed
½ x 325g block silken tofu,
   diced
A handful of frozen soybeans
85g bunch soba noodles,
   cooked and cooled under
   cold water
A pinch of finely chopped
   spring onion
1 tsp toasted sesame oil
Light soy sauce, to taste

Preheat your oven to 170°C (fan).

To make the shiitake 'bacon', lightly oil a baking sheet with some of the groundnut or vegetable oil. Mix any remaining oil with half the tamari or soy sauce and the maple syrup, and toss with the mushroom slices to coat. Lay the mushroom slices on the baking tray and sprinkle with the garlic powder, paprika, some sea salt and black pepper. Turn them over and lightly oil and season them again, then place them in the oven and bake for 40 minutes, turning the mushrooms halfway through cooking, until crisp.

While they're cooking, put the stock, ginger, seaweed and remaining tamari or soy in a pan and simmer for 10 minutes on a low-medium heat.

Towards the end of the shiitake mushrooms' cooking time, add the tofu, frozen soybeans and noodles to the broth to heat through. Pour into a soup bowl and top with the spring onion, shiitake 'bacon' and sesame oil. Season with light soy sauce, to taste.

SPICED CHICKPEAS AND CARROTS

●

Smoky paprika marries perfectly with sweet carrots here to give a satisfying but refreshing dinner bowl.

4 large carrots, peeled and cut into batons
Light olive oil
1 x 400g tin chickpeas, drained and rinsed
2 tsp cumin seeds
1 tsp smoked paprika
½ tsp sea salt, plus extra for seasoning
1 fennel bulb, very thinly sliced (on a mandoline is ideal)
Juice of ½ lemon
Extra-virgin olive oil (the same volume as the lemon juice)
A large pinch of finely chopped parsley
1 spring onion, thinly sliced
150g cooked freekeh, still warm
Tahini Goat's Yoghurt (see recipe on page 27)

Preheat your oven to 190°C (fan).

Parboil your carrots for 5 minutes, then drain. Lay them out on a baking tray and lightly drizzle them with oil, then add the chickpeas and sprinkle with the cumin seeds, paprika and the ½ teaspoon of sea salt. Bake for 20–30 minutes until the chickpeas have really coloured up and the carrots are turning brown at the edges. Shake the tray occasionally to turn them.

While they're cooking, add the fennel to a large bowl and separate the slices. Dress with the lemon juice, extra-virgin olive oil, parsley, spring onion and a scrunch of sea salt. Add the still-warm freekeh and mix.

Pile into a bowl and top with the hot chickpeas and carrots, drizzling with the Tahini Goat's Yoghurt.

SWEET POTATO FALAFEL

½ red pepper, diced
¼ cucumber, deseeded and
    diced
Juice of ½ lemon
Extra-virgin olive oil
    (the same volume as the
    lemon juice)
150g cooked farro, cooled
30g cooked green lentils, cooled
2 tbsp soybeans
1 tbsp chopped fresh coriander
    leaves and stalks
1 courgette, grated
Beetroot Yoghurt (see recipe
    on page 25)

For the soy-roasted linseeds:
1 tbsp soy sauce
2 tbsp groundnut oil
200g golden linseeds

*For the falafel (makes more than
you'll need for one bowl):*
800g sweet potatoes, roasted
    whole, in their skins, until
    just cooked, then cooled and
    peeled
150g gram flour
2 garlic cloves, peeled
A handful of fresh coriander
1 tsp ground cumin
1 tsp ground coriander
1 tsp smoked paprika
Sea salt and black pepper

Falafel, that Middle Eastern favourite, has taken over street markets and restaurant menus the world over in recent years. This sweet potato falafel bowl will leave you hungry for more – and luckily the recipe below makes enough falafels for more than one meal, so you can keep them in the fridge and munch on them throughout the week.

Preheat your oven to 160°C (fan).

First, make the soy-roasted linseeds. Mix together the soy and groundnut oil and pour it over the linseeds. Stir thoroughly to make sure all the seeds are covered, then smooth them out on a baking sheet, spreading them until they're as flat as possible. Bake for 20 minutes, stirring halfway through cooking. Remove from the oven once cooked and, once cooled, set aside in an airtight jar.

Increase the oven temperature to 180°C (fan).

To make the falafels, combine the sweet potatoes, gram flour, garlic, fresh coriander, ground cumin, ground coriander, smoked paprika and a generous scrunch of salt in a food processor and blitz until fairly smooth. Form the mixture into about 20–25 balls or quenelles and place on a lightly oiled baking sheet. Bake in the oven for 30 minutes, turning them once.

While they're cooking, mix the red pepper and cucumber together with the lemon juice and olive oil, season to taste and set aside. Then combine the farro with the green lentils, soybeans and coriander, and season with salt and pepper. When the falafels are cooked, serve hot with the cool farro, the pepper and cucumber mix, the courgette and the Beetroot Yoghurt, then sprinkle with the salty linseeds.

MISO AUBERGINE

●

Vegetable oil
1 large firm aubergine, halved
   lengthways and the flesh
   criss-crossed
2 tbsp brown miso paste
30ml water
125g block firm tofu, pressed
   and finely diced
1 tsp yuzu juice (or a mix of
   lime and mandarin juice if
   you can't find yuzu)
100g cooked black rice,
   warm or cold
100g cooked white rice,
   warm or cold
100g frozen soybeans or petits
   pois, thawed
1 spring onion, finely chopped
A handful of fresh coriander,
   chopped

For the miso dressing:
2 tbsp white miso paste
½ tsp toasted sesame oil
1 small garlic clove, finely
   chopped
Piece of fresh ginger, peeled
   and finely grated (to match
   the amount of garlic)
Juice of 1 lime
1 tbsp runny honey

The combination of miso and aubergine could not be any more perfect, and this bowl is so addictive you'll want to have it for dinner every day of the week.

First, make the miso dressing. In a bowl mix together the white miso paste, sesame oil, garlic and ginger, lime juice and honey. Set aside.

Preheat your oven to 160°C (fan). Lightly oil a baking sheet and place the aubergine halves on it. Mix the brown miso paste with the water to make a thick paste, then lightly brush the aubergines with oil followed by the brown miso paste. Cover with foil and bake for 30 minutes. Remove the foil, add the diced tofu to the sheet and bake for another 15 minutes. Remove from the oven and brush the yuzu over the aubergine flesh.

Mix the black and white rice with the thawed soybeans (or petits pois) and 1–2 tablespoons of the white miso dressing, then pile it all into a bowl and top with the aubergine and tofu. Finish with the sliced spring onion and coriander.

FRIED EGG ROMESCO

•

1 red pepper, diced
2 tbsp light olive oil
4–5 stalks of Tenderstem
broccoli
200g brown rice, cooked
in vegetable stock, and still
warm
Sunflower oil
1 egg
1 red chilli, deseeded and
deseeded and finely
chopped

For the soy-roasted linseeds:
See page 60

For the romesco sauce:
2 garlic cloves, still in their skins
1 slice of stale white bread,
diced
15g toasted skinned hazelnuts
1 level tsp smoked paprika
1 tbsp sherry vinegar
2 red peppers, blackened
under the grill and peeled
(jarred ones are fine)
100ml extra-virgin olive oil
Sea salt
Juice of ½ lemon

Enjoy the super-savoury hit from the paprika and sherry vinegar in this evening bowl, which is awash with Spanish flavours.

Preheat your oven to 160°C (fan).

Put the diced red pepper in a baking tray, drizzle with the olive oil and bake in the oven for 20 minutes until soft.

To make the romesco sauce, lightly oil the garlic cloves and bake on a baking tray for 20 minutes with the bread, until it starts to turn golden (this can be done at the same time as the diced red pepper). Remove from the oven and peel the garlic, putting it into a food processor with the bread, hazelnuts, smoked paprika, sherry vinegar, blackened red pepper flesh, olive oil and a pinch of salt to taste. Blitz until it forms a coarse paste. Taste for seasoning and add more salt if needed, and the lemon juice. Set aside.

Fill a pan with boiling water and simmer the broccoli for 4 minutes. During cooking, mix the warm brown rice with the roasted diced red peppers and pile into a bowl. Heat a frying pan on a high heat with a little sunflower oil and crack the egg in, fry for a couple of minutes, basting the yolk with the oil, then when the bottom of the egg starts to brown, remove and place on to the rice with the drained broccoli.

Top with a couple of tablespoons of the romesco sauce, a pinch of the chopped fresh red chilli and a scattering of soy-roasted linseeds.

ROASTED CAULIFLOWER AND CHIPOTLE

●

Once upon a time, cauliflower was the least cool of all vegetables. Now, liberated from the sole realm of Sunday dinner, it has taken on a new lease of life. Here, the humble vegetable is roasted in the oven and covered in addictive chipotle sauce – heavenly!

Olive oil

1 cauliflower head, cut into florets

Sea salt and black pepper

150g butternut squash, peeled and diced

1 raw beetroot, juiced, or 100ml shop-bought beetroot juice

1 cooked beetroot (not pickled!), peeled and diced

200g cooked white quinoa, warm or cold

Juice of ½ lemon

Chipotle Yoghurt (see recipe on page 25)

2 tbsp crushed pistachios

A handful of fresh radishes, sliced

A handful of sprouting seeds such as pea shoots

A handful of cooked and peeled broad beans and peas

Preheat your oven to 190°C (fan).

Lightly oil a baking tray and add the cauliflower florets. Add a drizzle of olive oil and season with salt, then bake in the oven for 40 minutes, turning the florets couple of times during cooking so the cauliflower starts to really colour up. During the last 20 minutes of cooking, add the diced squash to the baking tray to cook through.

While they're cooking, take the beetroot juice and diced beetroot and mix them through the cooked quinoa. Squeeze over the lemon juice, add a scrunch of sea salt and black pepper and set aside.

Serve the beetroot quinoa with the hot cauliflower and dressed in the Chipotle Yoghurt. Finish with the pistachios, radishes, sprouting seeds and broad beans and peas.

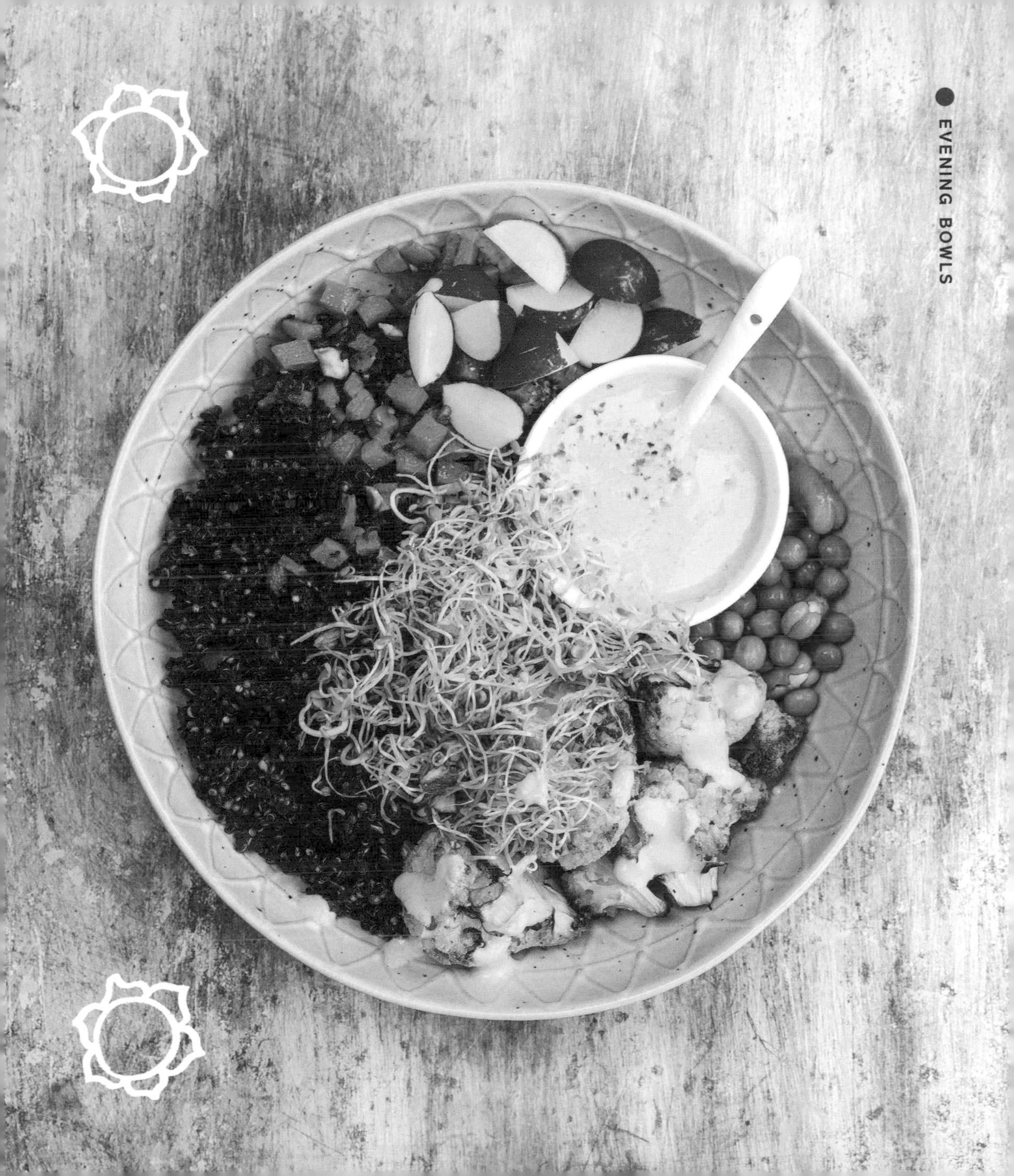

ROASTED CAULIFLOWER
AND TAHINI

●

**Don't let this super-simple bowl deceive you – it is full
of flavour and intriguing textures.**

Olive oil
1 cauliflower head, cut into
    florets
Sea salt
200g cooked puy lentils, cooled
100g feta,
    crumbled
Tahini Goat's Yoghurt
    (see recipe on page 27)
A handful of fresh mint leaves,
    finely chopped

Preheat your oven to 190°C (fan).

Lightly oil a baking tray and add the cauliflower florets. Drizzle them
in olive oil and season with salt, then bake in the oven for 40 minutes,
turning a couple of times during cooking so the cauliflower starts to
really colour up.

Pile the puy lentils into a bowl and add the hot cauliflower, then
crumble the feta over the top so it starts to melt. Drizzle the whole
bowl with the Tahini Goat's Yoghurt and scatter with the fresh mint.

RED ONION AND SWEET POTATO

●

**Who doesn't love the instantly satisfying taste of red onions?
Combine them with sweet potato and you've got the perfect
sweet and sticky combination.**

Olive oil

2 red onions, peeled and
quartered

200g tinned chickpeas,
drained and rinsed

1 sweet potato, parboiled
and diced

Sea salt and black pepper

1 broccoli head, cut into florets

A small handful of parsley,
finely chopped

200g cooked giant couscous,
cooled

Dijon Dressing (see recipe
on page 26)

2 tbsp toasted pine nuts

Preheat your oven to 190°C (fan).

Lightly oil a baking tray and add the red onions, chickpeas and sweet
potato, drizzling with a little olive oil and seasoning generously with
salt and pepper. Bake for 35 minutes, turning occasionally. Halfway
through cooking, add the broccoli florets to the baking tray – oil and
season these too and continue to bake until cooked through.

While the veg are cooking, mix the parsley through the giant couscous
and dress with 2 tablespoons of the Dijon Dressing and the pine
nuts. Pile the couscous into a bowl and top with the roasted veggies
and a little more of the Dijon Dressing.

Recovery Bowls

These bowls pack an extra punch of protein for those days
when your body really needs it – whether you're recovering
from a good workout or a heavy night out.

CUMIN CARROTS AND EGGS

Sweet carrots are offset by spicy chipotle yoghurt, fresh mint and zingy lemon in this light and colourful lunch bowl. Ideal for days when it's grey outside, its happy oranges and yellows will leave you with a summery feeling even in the depths of winter.

4 medium carrots, peeled and cut into batons
Light olive oil
Sea salt
1 tsp cumin seeds
200g cooked freekeh, cooled
1 preserved lemon, finely diced
A small handful of fresh mint, finely chopped, plus some whole leaves, to garnish
A handful of stoned black olives, squished
Extra-virgin olive oil
Juice of ½ lemon
White wine vinegar
2 eggs
½ avocado, peeled, stoned and sliced
A handful of sprouting nuts and seeds such as peanuts
1 tsp toasted crushed almonds
Chipotle Yoghurt (see recipe on page 25)

Preheat your oven to 190°C (fan).

Parboil the carrot batons in boiling water for 10 minutes, then rinse and drain. Place on a lightly oiled baking sheet and drizzle with a little olive oil and add a scrunch of salt. Bake for 35 minutes, turning occasionally, until the carrots start to colour up. Ten minutes before the carrots are done, sprinkle them with the cumin seeds.

In a bowl, mix together the cooked freekeh, preserved lemon, fresh mint, black olives and a glug of extra-virgin olive oil, season with salt and the lemon juice and set aside.

To poach the eggs, heat a pan of water and add a scrunch of salt and a dash of white wine vinegar. When it's at a rolling boil crack the eggs into the water and cook for 2 minutes for soft-poached eggs, then remove with a slotted spoon and place on kitchen paper to drain.

Pile the freekeh, carrots, avocado and sprouting nuts and seeds into a bowl and sprinkle with the toasted crushed almonds. Top with the poached eggs, a large dollop of Chipotle Yoghurt and a scrunch of salt.

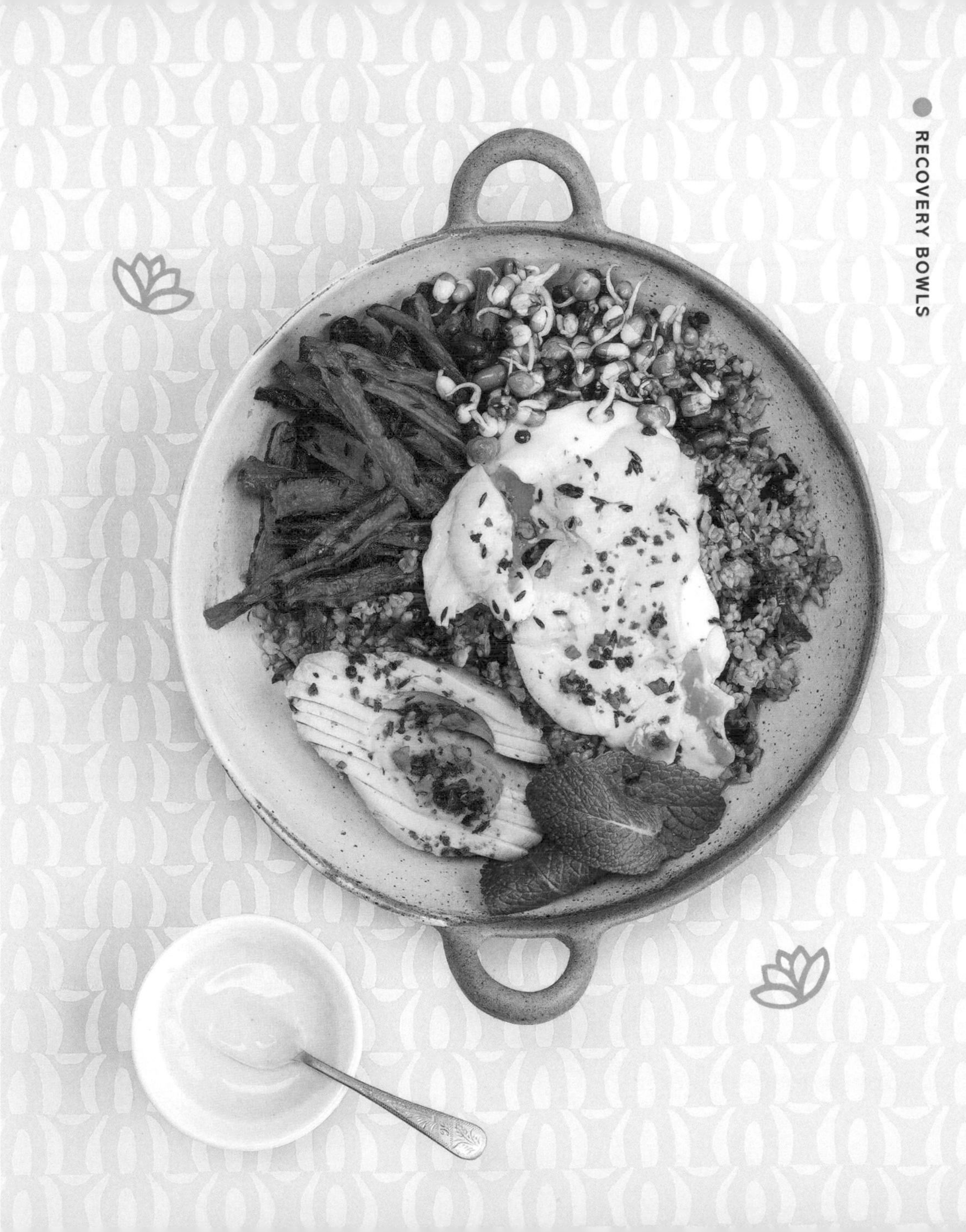

BEETROOT HUMMUS
AND BROCCOLI

●

**The colour combination of pink and green in this recipe
is immensely satisfying, as is the protein punch from
the chickpeas.**

Olive oil

1 medium broccoli head,
    cut into florets

1 garlic clove, sliced

½ red chilli, deseeded
    and finely chopped

Sea salt and black pepper

50ml Greek yoghurt

Juice of ½ lemon

1 tbsp diced peeled
    cucumber

100g cooked freekeh (cooked
    in vegetable stock), warm
    or cold

2 tbsp balsamic vinegar

A handful of fresh mint

For the beetroot hummus:

1 x 400g tin chickpeas, drained
    and rinsed

1 cooked beetroot (not
    pickled!), peeled and diced

2 tbsp tahini

2 garlic cloves, peeled

Juice of ½ lemon

100ml extra-virgin olive oil

Preheat your oven to 180°C (fan).

First, make the beetroot hummus. Place the chickpeas, beetroot, tahini, garlic, lemon juice and a generous scrunch of salt in a food processor. Blitz until smooth, then add the extra-virgin olive oil, blitz again and set aside in a bowl.

Lightly oil a baking tray and drizzle a little olive oil over the broccoli florets. Toss in a bowl with the garlic and chilli and a generous scrunch of sea salt and grind of black pepper, then lay out on the baking tray and bake for 15 minutes, turning twice.

Mix the yoghurt, lemon juice and cucumber together in a bowl and season with a little salt.

Pile the cooked freekeh into a serving bowl and top with the beetroot hummus. Remove the broccoli from the oven and drizzle with the vinegar, then add this to the bowl and finish with the yoghurt and a scattering of fresh mint.

BORLOTTI AND FETA

●

**The humble borlotti bean is transformed here into a sort
of vegetarian/Mediterranean take on the Waldorf salad.**

200g tinned borlotti beans,
  drained and rinsed
150g just-cooked buckwheat
  groats, warm
A large handful of sprouting
  seeds
4 tbsp Dijon Dressing
  (see recipe on page 26)
100g feta, crumbled
A handful of walnut halves
A handful of green grapes, halved
1 tsp toasted sesame seeds

Warm the borlotti beans in boiling water for 3 minutes, then drain. In a mixing bowl, combine the beans with the buckwheat groats, sprouting seeds, Dijon Dressing, crumbled feta, walnuts and grapes. Pile it all into a serving bowl, and top with the toasted sesame seeds.

HALLOUMI AND TZATZIKI

●

**After a heavy workout you deserve some halloumi,
and after a heavy night out you just need it. This is
a bowl for both eventualities.**

Olive oil
250g block halloumi, thickly
   sliced
½ red pepper, diced
¼ red onion, peeled and
   finely chopped
1 x 400g tin chickpeas,
   drained and rinsed
100g cooked couscous,
   warm or cold
1 Little Gem lettuce, finely
   shredded

For the tzatziki:
150ml Greek yoghurt
¼ cucumber, deseeded,
   peeled and diced
½ garlic clove, finely chopped
1 tbsp lemon juice
1 tbsp olive oil
A pinch of fresh mint leaves,
   finely chopped
Sea salt

Heat a frying pan on a medium-high heat and add a little olive oil for
cooking. Add the halloumi slices to the pan and cook for 2–3 minutes
on each side until lightly golden.

While that's cooking, make the tzatziki. Mix together the yoghurt,
cucumber, garlic, lemon juice, olive oil, mint and a generous pinch
of sea salt in a bowl.

Add the red pepper, onion, chickpeas and couscous to a serving bowl
and stir together. Top with the halloumi, shredded lettuce and tzatziki.

PANEER AND BELUGA LENTILS

•

Paneer is the new halloumi. Still slightly less popular on UK restaurant menus, this Indian cheese, like its Greek counterpart, is deliciously salty and creamy, with a wonderful texture that soaks up flavours. A perfect accompaniment to intense sriracha and soy sauce!

225g block paneer, diced
Groundnut or sunflower oil
200g cooked beluga lentils, cooled
2 tbsp Dijon Dressing (see recipe on page 26)
1 large carrot, spiralised or shredded
A small handful of fresh mint, shredded
Sriracha, to taste

For the soy-roasted seeds:
2 tbsp groundnut or sunflower oil
1 tbsp light soy sauce
200g pumpkin and sunflower seeds

Preheat your oven to 160°C (fan).

First, make the soy-roasted seeds. Mix the oil and soy sauce together in a bowl and pour over the seeds, stirring thoroughly to coat. Spread over a lined baking tray and bake for 20 minutes, stirring with a fork halfway through cooking. Remove and set aside to cool – this delicious snack keeps well in an airtight jar and works well on bowls of all kinds.

Preheat your griddle for 5 minutes on a high heat and lightly coat the diced paneer in some groundnut or sunflower oil. Place the paneer on the griddle and cook for about 8 minutes, turning occasionally until it colours.

Dress the beluga lentils in the Dijon Dressing and place in a bowl with the carrot, mint and 3 tablespoons of the soy-roasted seeds. Finish with the hot paneer and sriracha.

CHILLI OMELETTE

●

This is a great meal to whip up after a workout or at the end of a long day, when you need nourishment and flavour fast and don't want to spend hours over the stove. Perfectly balanced and packed with protein, it's the ultimate comfort Buddha Bowl.

1 red chilli, deseeded and finely chopped

2 eggs, lightly beaten and seasoned with salt

Groundnut or sunflower oil

1 large cooked beetroot (not pickled!), peeled and spiralised or shredded

Juice of ½ lime

Extra-virgin olive oil (the same volume as the lime juice)

Sea salt and black pepper

200g cooked brown rice (cooked in vegetable stock), warm

A pinch of sprouting shoots

½ avocado, peeled, stoned and sliced

Smoky Carrot Sauce (see recipe on page 27)

Soy-Roasted Linseeds (see recipe on page 60)

Mix the chilli into the beaten egg. Heat a little groundnut or sunflower oil in a frying pan on a medium heat, and pour in the egg mixture. Turn the omelette over after a couple of minutes and turn off the heat; the egg will cook through in the residual heat.

Mix the spiralised beetroot with the lime juice and the same amount of extra-virgin olive oil, season with salt and pepper and add to a bowl with the brown rice and shoots.

Cut the omelette into triangles and add to the bowl with the avocado, Smoky Carrot Sauce and 2 tablespoons of the soy-roasted linseeds.

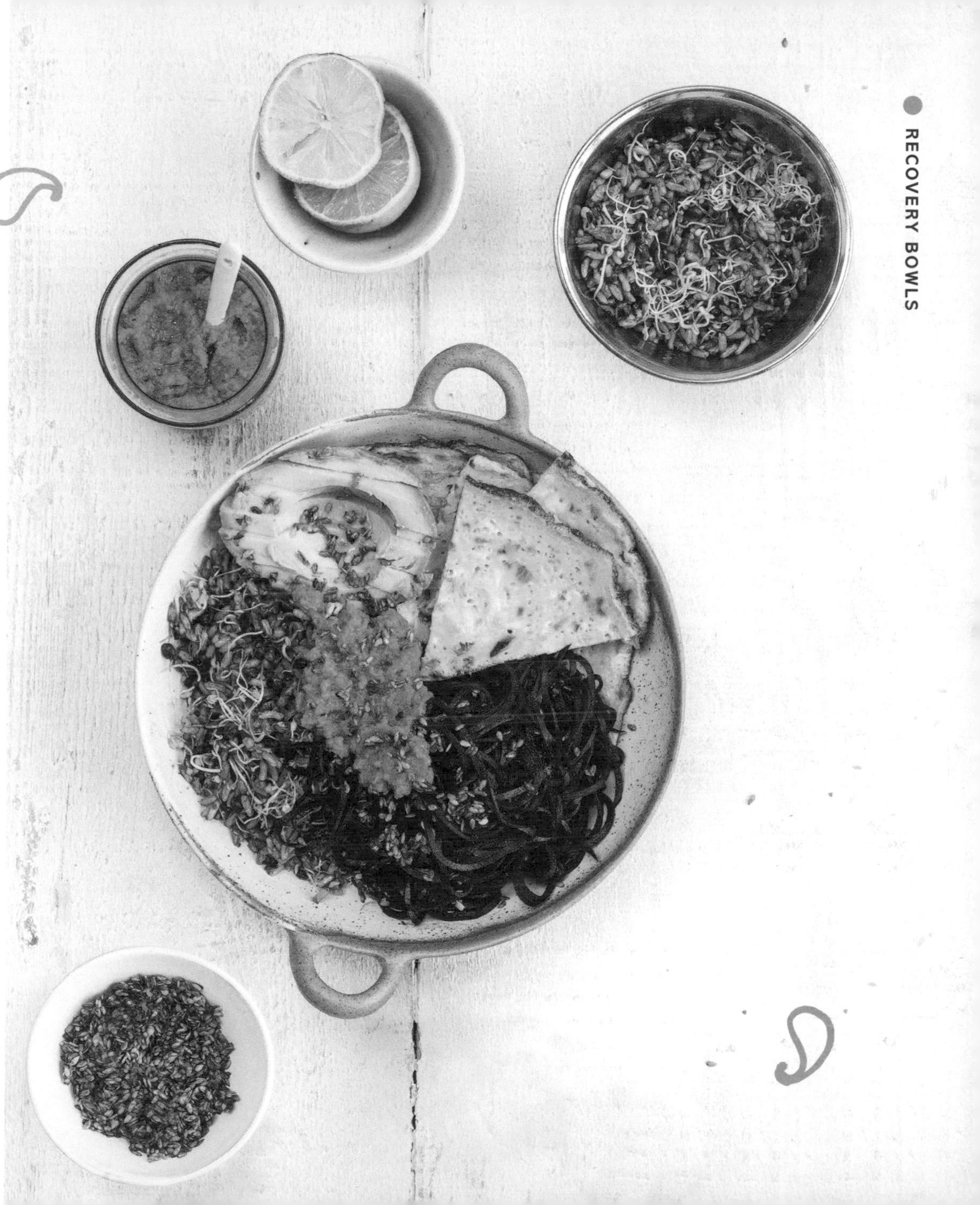

ZA'ATAR SQUASH

Za'atar is the one spice mix ready to take over everyone's
spice cupboards. Salty and full of flavour, here it combines
with soft and delicious squash for a bowl that will restore
and revive you.

Olive oil
1 small butternut squash,
    peeled, deseeded and diced
2 tsp za'atar spice mix
Sea salt and black pepper
1 red onion, peeled and
    quartered
A handful of kale, finely
    shredded and blanched
    in boiling water for 1 minute
Juice of 1 lemon
1 tsp toasted nigella seeds
200g tinned chickpeas,
    drained and rinsed
150g giant couscous
Tahini Goat's Yoghurt
    (see recipe on page 27)

Preheat your oven to 180°C (fan).

Lightly oil the diced squash, spread it out on a baking tray and scatter
with the za'atar, a scrunch of sea salt and a generous grind of black
pepper so they're coated all over. Roast in the oven for 30–40
minutes. After 15 minutes of cooking, add the onion quarters to the
baking tray and shake to mix. Cook until soft and the edges have
started to char.

Towards the end of cooking, mix the drained kale, lemon juice and
nigella seeds with the chickpeas and giant couscous in a bowl and
season with salt and pepper. Pile into a bowl and top with the roasted
squash, onion and a big spoon of Tahini Goat's Yoghurt.

SMOKY SOBA NOODLES

**Enjoy smoky and satisfying flavours in this bowl.
The recipe for the almonds makes more than you'll need,
but feel free to pile them on or use them as an extra snack!**

85g soba noodles, cooked,
   drained and set aside
1 large courgette, spiralised
   or grated
Finely grated zest of
   ½ unwaxed lemon
Chipotle Yoghurt (see recipe
   on page 25)

For the smoky almonds:*
100g almonds, skin on
1 tbsp groundnut oil
1 heaped tsp smoked paprika
1 tsp sea salt

First, make the smoky almonds.

Preheat your oven to 190°C (fan).

Place the almonds and groundnut oil in a mixing bowl to coat, then
lay them flat on a baking tray and bake for 10 minutes, shaking the
tray once. Remove from the oven and sprinkle with the smoked
paprika and sea salt, mixing together thoroughly. Let the nuts cool.
Take 3 tablespoons of the smoky almonds and pulse in a food
processor until roughly crushed.

Reheat the noodles in boiling water for a couple of minutes and
drain. Mix with the crushed smoky almonds and toss through with
the spiralised courgette and lemon zest. Pile into a bowl and top
with a dollop of the Chipotle Yoghurt.

*This makes more
than the recipe
needs, but they keep
well in an airtight
container

BANG BANG HALLOUMI

●

This recipe is absolutely bang on. Zingy flavours from the lemon and the Bang Bang Dressing are soaked up by the deliciously soft and sweet halloumi.

125g halloumi, cut into
  chunky batons
Groundnut or sunflower oil
Several Tenderstem broccoli
  stalks
100g cooked farro, warm
100g cooked green lentils,
  warm
A handful of kale, finely
  shredded
1 tbsp soybeans
Sea salt and black pepper
Juice of ½ lemon, plus extra
  for dressing
A handful of shredded red
  cabbage
Extra-virgin olive oil
Bang Bang Dressing
  (see recipe on page 22)
A pinch of black sesame seeds

Heat your griddle on a high heat for at least 5 minutes.

Lightly coat the halloumi in groundnut or sunflower oil and cook on the bars until they're turning golden on each side.

While the halloumi is cooking, simmer the broccoli in a pan of boiling water for about 4 minutes until just cooked through, then drain it and plunge it into cold water to cool. Drain again and set aside.

Mix together the farro and lentils in a bowl with the kale and soybeans, and season with salt, pepper and lemon juice. Dress the red cabbage in a little extra-virgin olive oil, lemon juice and salt, then pile into a bowl with the farro and lentil mixture, broccoli and halloumi. Finish with a couple of tablespoons of the Bang Bang Dressing and a sprinkle of black sesame seeds.

Quicker-Than-a-Takeaway Bowls

These quick and tasty bowls are inspired by the flavours of all of your favourite takeaways, from Chinese to Indian to the inimitable piri piri. They provide the same enjoyment but tonnes more nutrients, so you can feel good while slobbing on the sofa, indulging in a bowl of hearty goodness.

SWEET AND SOUR TOFU

•

Tofu often gets a bad rep, but, like so many things, it can be evil or wonderfully good depending on what you choose to do with it. Here, the tangy marinade seeps into the tofu, giving it a rich, lip-smacking flavour that is perfectly complemented by the powerful Bang Bang Dressing.

250g block firm tofu, drained, pressed and diced*
Vegetable oil
½ red pepper, cut into large chunks
½ yellow pepper, cut into large chunks
4–5 Tenderstem broccoli stalks
200g cooked basmati rice (warm or cold)
A handful of radishes, quartered
Bang Bang Dressing (see recipe on page 22)
A few fresh coriander leaves

For the marinade:
3 tbsp light soy sauce
3 tbsp rice vinegar
3 tbsp agave syrup or runny honey
1 tbsp tomato ketchup

Preheat your oven to 180°C (fan).

To make the marinade, mix the soy sauce, rice vinegar, agave or honey and ketchup in a bowl and add in the diced tofu. Set aside for at least an hour before cooking.

Lightly oil a baking tray and add the chopped peppers, tossing to coat lightly in the oil. Bake in the oven for 40 minutes until softened and starting to char around the edges, then remove and set aside.

Set your grill to its highest heat, then line a baking sheet with foil and lightly oil. Place the marinated tofu pieces on the foil and grill under the high heat for about 20 minutes, turning them occasionally when the edges start to really colour up.

Towards the end of cooking the peppers and tofu, simmer the broccoli stalks for 4–5 minutes until just cooked through, then drain.

Place the cooked rice in a serving bowl, followed by the hot tofu, broccoli, peppers, radishes and a few spoonfuls of the Bang Bang Dressing. Garnish with a few coriander leaves.

*To press tofu, simply press it between two plates, with a weight on top, to remove excess water.

PIRI PIRI TOFU

●

Everyone loves the spicy, tangy flavours of piri piri. Here, they meet tofu to create an excitingly flavoured bowl of goodness that is every bit as tasty as its high-street chicken-shop equivalent.

3 tbsp piri piri paste
100ml Greek yoghurt
250g block firm tofu, drained, pressed and finely sliced*
Groundnut or vegetable oil
1 corn cob
¼ red cabbage, finely shredded
¼ white cabbage, finely shredded
Juice of 1 lime
200g cooked brown rice, cooled
Avocado Lime Crema (see recipe on page 22)

Preheat your oven to 200°C (fan).

Mix the piri piri paste with the yoghurt in a bowl and coat the tofu with it. Place the tofu slices on a lightly oiled baking sheet and bake in the oven for 30 minutes, turning them occasionally.

Halfway through cooking, preheat your griddle on a high heat and let it warm for 5 minutes. Lightly oil the corn cob and place on the griddle, turning the cob occasionally for 6–8 minutes until it's lightly charred. Remove from the heat and leave until cool enough to be handled.

Mix the red and white cabbage with the lime juice and pile into your serving bowl with the brown rice and hot tofu. Slice the corn kernels from the cob and add to the bowl and dress with Avocado Lime Crema.

*To press tofu, simply press it between two plates, with a weight on top, to remove excess water.

MEXICAN SQUASH

All the best flavours of Mexico combine here, alongside a whole garden of vegetables, to create a healthy Buddha-Bowls take on tacos.

Olive oil
1 small butternut squash, peeled and diced
1 tsp ground cumin
1 tsp ground coriander
½ tsp smoked paprika
½ tsp ground cayenne pepper
Sea salt and black pepper
1 Little Gem lettuce, shredded
½ avocado, peeled, stoned and sliced
200g flaxseed crackers
A handful of fresh coriander, stalks discarded
2 spring onions, finely chopped
Juice of ½ lime
Chipotle Yoghurt (see recipe on page 25)

Preheat your oven to 180°C (fan).

Lightly oil the squash chunks and spread them out on a baking tray. Mix the ground spices together with a scrunch of sea salt and a generous grind of black pepper. Scatter over the spice blend and mix so the squash is coated. Bake in the oven for 30–40 minutes until the squash is soft and the edges have started to char.

Fill a bowl with the shredded lettuce and layer up with the avocado, flaxseed crackers (for scooping) and hot squash. Top with the coriander, spring onions and lime juice and a big dollop of Chipotle Yoghurt.

THAI-STYLE TOFU

•

Lighter than a pad Thai but with all the same aromatic notes of limes, coriander, peanuts and soy sauce, this Thai-style Tofu will satisfy your takeaway cravings!

80g flat rice noodles, cooked and cooled
Groundnut or sunflower oil
250g block firm tofu, drained, pressed and thinly sliced*
10 chestnut mushrooms, brushed of any dirt (but not washed) and halved
2 tbsp toasted peanuts
¼ cucumber, thinly sliced into rounds
1 radish, thinly sliced
2 spring onions, thinly sliced
A few sprigs of fresh coriander
A splash of sriracha

For the dressing:
2 tbsp lime juice
2 tbsp dark brown sugar
2 tbsp light soy sauce
1 tsp toasted sesame oil

Preheat your oven to 200°C (fan).

First, make the dressing. Mix the lime juice, sugar, soy sauce and sesame oil together in a bowl and pour half of it over the cooked noodles. Set the noodles aside and retain the rest of the dressing to use later.

Oil a baking tray and lay the tofu slices out on it, brushing the slices with some more oil, and put the halved mushrooms alongside them. Bake in the oven until the mushrooms are softened and the tofu is browned and crisp at the edges – around 20–30 minutes.

Towards the end of cooking, pile the noodles into your serving bowl. Top with the mushrooms, tofu, nuts, cucumber, radish, spring onions and coriander, and spoon over the remaining dressing. Finish with a splash of fiery sriracha.

*To press tofu, simply press it between two plates, with a weight on top, to remove excess water.

QUICKER-THAN-A-TAKEAWAY BOWLS

MUSHROOM NOODLES

Noodles are a mainstay of the takeaway diet, and these ones are full of sticky, earthy flavours that are sure to kick the craving.

Vegetable oil
200g chestnut mushrooms, brushed of any dirt (but not washed) and halved
2 tbsp runny honey
1 tsp finely chopped garlic
1 tsp peeled and grated ginger
½ tsp sriracha
1 tbsp lime juice
1 tsp soy sauce
85g soba noodles, cooked according to packet instructions
100g fresh spinach, finely chopped
Soy-roasted Seeds (see page 88)

Preheat your oven to 180°C (fan).

Lightly oil a baking sheet, add the mushrooms to it and bake for 25 minutes. While they're cooking, mix together the honey, garlic and ginger, sriracha, lime juice and soy sauce in a bowl to make a dressing.

Reheat the noodles by soaking them in boiling water in the last 5 minutes of the mushroom baking time. Drain the noodles and add to the dressing bowl, turning them over until they're completely coated, then add the chopped spinach to the bowl and mix again.

Pile the noodles into a serving bowl and top with the mushrooms and Soy-roasted seeds.

SHIITAKE 'BACON' AND EGGS

Okay, so bacon and eggs might not be a takeaway favourite, but they are a greasy-spoon, breakfast-for-dinner love for many of us, so this nourishing alternative finds its way into the takeaway chapter to help you out when you just need something salty, satisfying and deliciously good for you.

15 shiitake mushrooms, thinly sliced
A pinch of garlic powder
¼ tsp smoked paprika
Sea salt and black pepper
A vine of cherry tomatoes
2 portobello mushrooms
3 tsp groundnut or vegetable oil, plus extra for cooking
2 tsp maple syrup
6 tsp tamari or soy sauce
½ tsp rice vinegar
200g cooked black or beluga lentils
2 eggs

Preheat your oven to 170°C (fan).

Lightly oil a baking tray and place the shiitake mushrooms on it. Lightly oil them and sprinkle with the garlic powder and paprika. Season to taste with sea salt and black pepper, then turn them over and lightly oil and season them again. Place them in the oven and bake for 40 minutes, turning them halfway through cooking. On a separate baking tray, lightly oil the tomatoes and portobello mushrooms and roast them (mushrooms cap side up) for the same amount of time.

While the mushrooms and tomatoes are cooking, add the groundnut or vegetable oil, maple syrup, tamari or soy sauce and rice vinegar to a large bowl and mix together well to make a dressing.

During the last 5 minutes of cooking, reheat the lentils in boiling water.

Remove the shiitake mushrooms from the oven and put them in the bowl with the dressing. Turn them in the dressing so they're all covered, then set aside.

Heat a frying pan over a medium-high heat and add a glug of groundnut or vegetable oil for cooking. When the oil is lightly shimmering, crack in the eggs and season with salt and pepper. Fry until the whites are looking firm and baste the yolks with a little of the oil in the pan. Take the pan off the heat.

Drain the lentils and pile into a bowl. Top with the roast portobello mushrooms, tomatoes, eggs and 'bacon'.

TANDOORI PANEER

●

This Tandoori Paneer is brought to life by a zingy chopped salad with lemon, while a creamy cucumber labneh cuts through the spices. Taking just moments to put together, this will be on your table and in your mouth quicker than the takeaway dish that inspired it.

4 tbsp full-fat natural yoghurt
2 tbsp tandoori paste
225g block paneer, diced
Vegetable oil
200g cooked farro, cooled
1 tbsp fresh coriander, chopped
A handful of fresh spinach
2 tbsp toasted chopped nuts
    such as peanuts, cashews
    or almonds

For the salad:
½ red pepper, diced
½ yellow pepper, diced
½ cucumber, deseeded and
    diced
¼ red onion, peeled and
    finely diced
Juice of ½ lemon, plus extra
    to serve
50ml extra-virgin olive oil
Sea salt and black pepper

For the cucumber labneh:
100ml labneh or Greek yoghurt
½ cucumber, deseeded and
    diced
Juice of ½ lemon or lime

First, mix together the yoghurt and tandoori paste in a bowl and coat the paneer, then leave it to marinate for at least 2 hours or up to 1 day.

To make the salad, mix the peppers, cucumber, red onion, lemon juice and extra-virgin olive oil together in a bowl. Add sea salt and pepper to taste and set aside.

To make the cucumber labneh, mix the labneh or Greek yoghurt, cucumber and lemon or lime juice together in a bowl and set aside in the fridge.

Preheat your grill to its highest heat. Line a baking sheet with foil and lightly oil, then place the marinated paneer pieces on the foil and grill under the high heat for about 20 minutes, turning the pieces occasionally when the edges start to really colour up.

Mix the farro and coriander and place it with the spinach in a serving bowl, followed by the chopped salad, the hot paneer, cucumber labneh and toasted nuts. Give the paneer a good squeeze of lemon before tucking in.

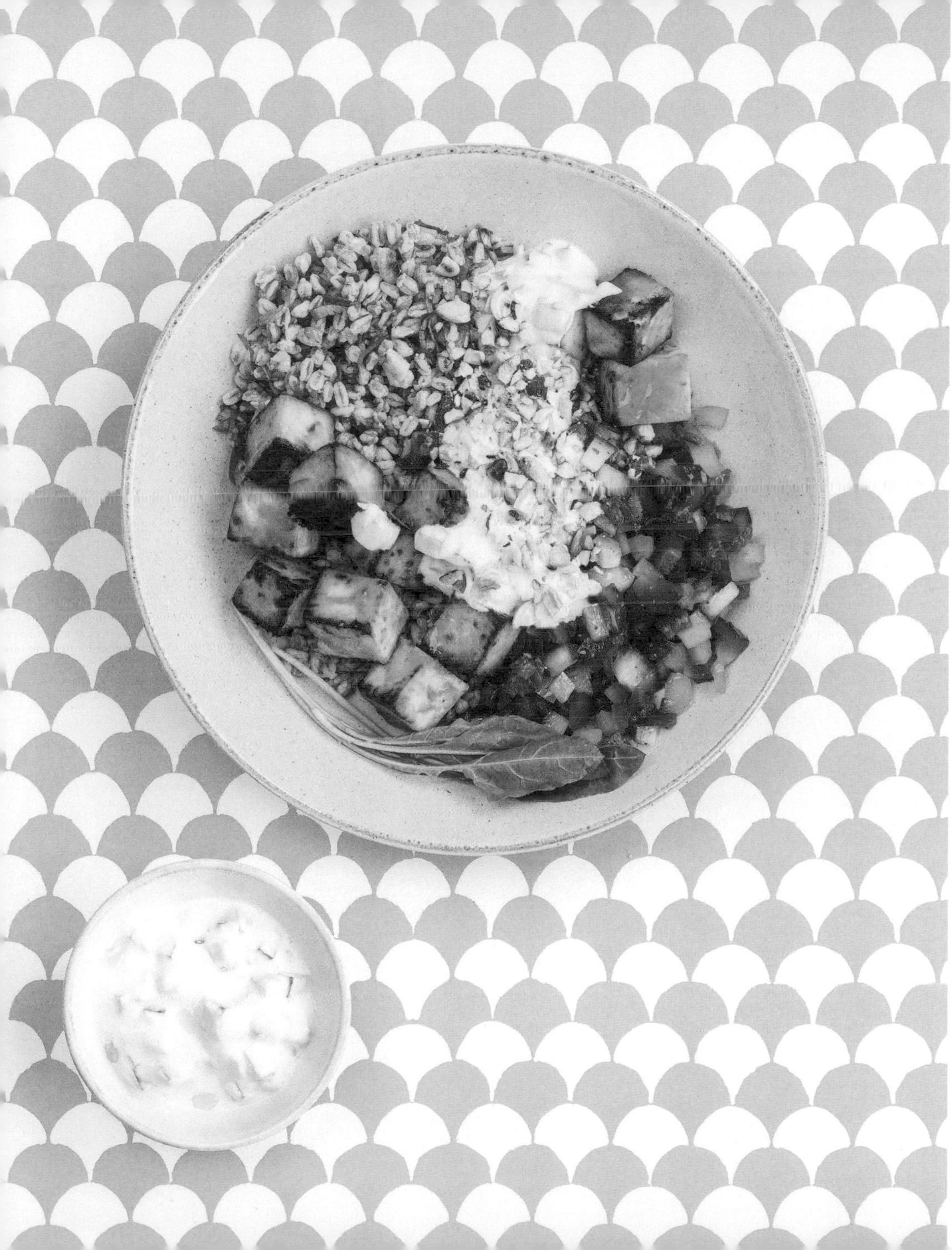

Dinner Party Bowls

These are the bowls that are perfect for sharing or serving up to your nearest and dearest as part of an intimate dinner party. Taking inspiration from flavours around the world, they call on the culinary expertise of everywhere from France to Greece to the Middle East. Each recipe makes a single bowl, so just multiply amounts for however many people you're cooking for.

DHAL AND CUMIN CARROTS

●

**This dhal is sure to become a favourite – the pleasing
orange colour creates a happy bowl of food.**

100g yellow split peas
4 medium carrots, peeled and
   cut into batons
Olive oil
Sea salt
1 tbsp cumin seeds
1 small red onion, finely chopped
1 tsp grated or finely
   chopped ginger
1 tsp finely chopped garlic
1 tsp ground cumin
1 tsp ground coriander
1 tsp ground turmeric
½ green chilli, deseeded
   and finely chopped
1 tomato, diced
200ml vegetable stock
100g baby spinach
Juice of 1 lime
2 tbsp natural yoghurt
A handful of fresh coriander
1 tsp cumin seeds

Preheat your oven to 190°C (fan).

Rinse the yellow split peas and soak them in a large pot of cold
water for 30 minutes.

Pre-cook the carrot batons in boiling water for 10 minutes, then
drain. Place on a lightly oiled baking sheet, drizzle with a little olive oil
and give a scrunch of salt. Bake for 35 minutes, turning occasionally,
until the carrots start to colour up. Ten minutes before the end of the
cooking time, add the cumin seeds and toss to combine, returning the
baking sheet to the oven.

While the carrots are cooking, add a little oil to a saucepan and cook
down the onion on a low-medium heat until really soft. Add the ginger,
garlic, ground cumin, ground coriander, ground turmeric, and green
chilli and continue to cook for a few minutes, followed by the diced
tomato and the split peas. Add the stock and bring to the boil. Skim
off any scum that forms on the top as the split peas cook and discard.
Reduce to a simmer and cook for 40 minutes until the split peas are
soft. Remove from the heat and beat with a whisk to break the split
peas down. Add the spinach and allow it to wilt. Season with salt to
taste and add the lime juice.

Pile into a serving bowl, top with the roasted carrots and finish with
the yoghurt and coriander.

CHARRED CORN
AND GUACAMOLE

●

This is the Buddha-Bowls take on tacos – all the Mexican flavours with a bit of what's good for you, too.

Olive oil
1 sweet potato, peeled
   and diced
1 corn cob
A handful of shredded red
   cabbage
A handful of fresh coriander
1 tbsp cashews, toasted and
   roughly chopped

For the guacamole:
1 avocado, peeled, stoned
   and lightly mashed
1 tomato, deseeded and
   finely diced
¼ small red onion, finely diced
A pinch of chopped fresh
   red chilli
½ garlic clove, finely chopped
Juice of 1 lime
Sea salt

Preheat your oven to 190°C (fan).

Lightly oil a baking tray, add the diced sweet potato, drizzle with a little oil and and bake for 20–30 minutes until softened, turning the sweet potato occasionally.

While that's cooking, preheat your griddle for 5 minutes over a high heat. Lightly oil the corn cob, place it on the bars and allow to char, turning the corn regularly to get each side coloured and to cook the corn through.

To make the guacamole, mix the avocado, tomato, red onion, red chilli, garlic, lime juice and a pinch of salt together in a bowl.

When the corn's cool enough to handle, cut the kernels off the cob and mix them through the rice. Pile the mix into a bowl and top with the sweet potato, red cabbage, coriander, guacamole and chopped cashews.

PERSIAN AUBERGINE

●

Everyone knows aubergine and pomegranate seeds look beautiful in a bowl together, and the fresh flavours of mint and coriander punch through the the softer flavours in this bowl to create something that tastes as good as it looks.

Sunflower or groundnut oil
4 baby aubergines or 1 regular
 aubergine, cut into rounds
1 tsp baharat spice mix
Sea salt
½ red pepper, finely diced
½ green pepper, finely diced
½ yellow pepper, finely diced
3 medium–large tomatoes,
 deseeded and finely diced
¼ cucumber, deseeded and
 finely diced
½ small red onion, finely diced
Juice of 1 lemon
Extra-virgin olive oil (the same
 volume as the lemon juice)
A small handful of fresh mint
 leaves, half finely shredded
200g cooked white quinoa,
 cooled
2 tbsp pomegranate molasses
2 tbsp date syrup
A few fresh coriander leaves
Seeds from ½ pomegranate

Preheat your oven to 180°C (fan) and lightly oil a baking sheet.

Slice the aubergines in half lengthways, lightly oiling them and then sprinkling them with the baharat spice mix followed by a little salt. Place cut side down on the baking sheet and cook for 30–40 minutes until the flesh is soft and they've browned on their cut side, turning them once during cooking.

While they're cooking, mix together the diced peppers, tomatoes, cucumber and onion in a bowl and pour over the lemon juice and extra-virgin olive oil. Add a generous scrunch of salt, mixing thoroughly and tasting and adjusting the seasoning if needed.

Mix the shredded mint leaves with the cooked quinoa and pile into a serving bowl, topping with the chopped salad so all the juices mingle with the grains.

Mix the pomegranate molasses and date syrup together until combined. Remove the aubergine from the oven and add to the serving bowl. Spoon over the pomegranate and date dressing, and finish with the remaining mint leaves, the coriander and the pomegranate seeds.

SPICY PAELLA

•

**Transport yourself to Spain with this delicious paella,
which keeps its balance between all elements of the
Buddha Bowl and the addition of fresh raw veggies
such as radishes.**

Olive oil
250g block silken tofu
1 tbsp runny honey
1 tsp toasted sesame seeds
1 tbsp soy sauce
1 red onion, diced
1 red pepper, deseeded and
    diced
1 garlic clove, finely chopped
150g white rice
300ml vegetable stock, boiling
Juice of ½ lemon
100g frozen peas
A handful of fresh parsley,
    chopped
1 tsp smoked paprika
½ red chilli, diced
1 carrot, spiralised, coarsely
    grated or shredded
4 radishes, thinly sliced,
    then cut into matchsticks
A handful of fresh basil leaves

Preheat your oven to 190°C (fan).

Lightly oil a baking tray and lay the block of tofu in it. Mix the honey, sesame seeds and soy sauce together, then coat the tofu in the mixture and bake for 20 minutes.

Meanwhile, cook the onion and red pepper in a saucepan with a little olive oil over a medium heat for 8–10 minutes and, when soft, add the garlic and rice and cook for a further. Add the boiling stock and stir, then reduce the heat to its lowest setting, put the lid on the pan and cook for 15 minutes.

Remove from the heat and add the lemon juice, peas, parsley, paprika and chilli. Cover the pan with a towel for 5 minutes. Pile it all into a bowl with the carrot and scoop the tofu over the top, scatter with the radish and basil and serve.

SUNDRIED-TOMATO
AUBERGINE

●

**Enjoy all the flavours of Provence in this rich,
tomato-based dinner party bowl.**

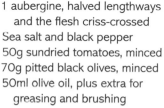

1 aubergine, halved lengthways
  and the flesh criss-crossed
Sea salt and black pepper
50g sundried tomatoes, minced
70g pitted black olives, minced
50ml olive oil, plus extra for
  greasing and brushing
1 vine of cherry tomatoes
2 large handfuls of kale, finely
  chopped
3 tbsp Dijon Dressing
  (see recipe on page 26)
200g cooked giant couscous,
  warm
A squeeze of lemon
2 tbsp toasted pine nuts
A small handful of fresh parsley,
  chopped

Preheat your oven to 190°C (fan).

Lightly oil a baking tray and lay out the aubergine slices on it. Brush with a little olive oil, season with salt and pepper and then bake for 20 minutes.

Mix the sundried tomatoes and black olives together with the olive oil and spoon the mixture over the aubergine slices. Return the tray to the oven and bake for a further 12–15 minutes. Lightly oil the vine tomatoes and place them on a separate baking tray in the oven for the same amount of time.

Mix the kale and Dijon Dressing through the couscous and pile into a bowl. Top with the baked aubergine, then add a squeeze of lemon juice and scatter with the pine nuts and parsley.

STICKY SWEET POTATO

•

**Enjoy a little taste of Morocco in this sweet and sticky bowl,
which is ideal for serving up on a warm summer's evening.**

1 large sweet potato, peeled
and diced
Groundnut or vegetable oil
1 tsp ground cumin
1 tsp ground coriander
A pinch of chilli flakes
Sea salt
Juice of 1 lime
¼ white cabbage, finely
shredded
¼ red cabbage, finely
shredded
200g cooked brown rice,
warm or cold
200g tinned chickpeas,
drained and rinsed
2 tbsp date syrup
½ tsp sriracha
2 tbsp goat's yoghurt
A small handful of pistachios
A small handful of fresh
coriander

Preheat your oven to 180°C (fan).

While the oven is warming, parboil the diced sweet potato in
water for 5 minutes. Drain and then transfer to a baking tray.
Lightly drizzle with the groundnut or vegetable oil and sprinkle
over the cumin, ground coriander and chilli flakes, mixing it all
so the potato is coated. Sprinkle with salt and bake for around
30 minutes.

Towards the end of the cooking time, mix half the lime juice
through the white and red cabbage, and then pile it all into
a serving bowl with the brown rice and chickpeas.

Mix the date syrup together with the sriracha and remaining
lime juice in a bowl until combined. Remove the sweet potato
from the oven and add to the serving bowl. Spoon over the
goat's yoghurt and sticky date sauce, finishing with the
pistachios and coriander.

SMOKED TOFU

•

**This smoky and spicy tofu is ideal
for casual entertaining.**

2 cooked beetroot
   (not pickled!), peeled
150g smoked tofu
2 slices pumpernickel rye bread
¼ cucumber, deseeded and
   sliced
A handful of fresh spinach
Dijon Dressing
   (see recipe on page 26)
Greek yoghurt
A handful of dried
   cranberries

Quarter the beetroots and then halve them again.

Cut the tofu into slices and then halve into triangles, and cut the
pumpernickel bread into triangles, too.

Layer up in a bowl with the cucumber and fresh spinach, then drizzle
with a couple of tablespoons of the Dijon Dressing and Greek yoghurt
and sprinkle the dried cranberries on top.

COCONUT TOFU

●

**Coconut alongside ginger brings a creamy yet
refreshing combination of Thai-inspired flavours
to this protein-rich bowl.**

Groundnut or vegetable oil
100ml coconut milk
1 tbsp soy sauce
1 garlic clove, finely chopped
1 tbsp minced ginger
1 tbsp rice vinegar
100ml natural or Greek yoghurt
1 block firm tofu, drained,
    pressed and diced*
200g cooked white rice, warm
    or cold
1 large carrot, spiralised or
    grated
Bang Bang Dressing
    (see recipe on page 22)
A handful of fresh coriander
¼ cucumber, deseeded, peeled
    and diced
50g fresh coconut chunks
2 spring onions, finely chopped
1 red chilli, deseeded and
    finely chopped (optional)

Preheat your oven to 190°C (fan).

Lightly oil a baking tray and mix together the coconut milk, soy sauce, garlic, ginger, rice vinegar and yoghurt in a bowl. Coat the diced tofu in the mixture and lay out on a baking tray. Bake for 20–25 minutes, turning occasionally.

Pile the rice and spiralised carrot into a serving bowl and top with the hot tofu. Drizzle with Bang Bang Dressing and scatter with the coriander leaves and diced cucumber. Finish with coconut chunks, spring onions and chilli (to taste).

*To press tofu,
simply press it
between two plates,
with a weight on top,
to remove excess
water.

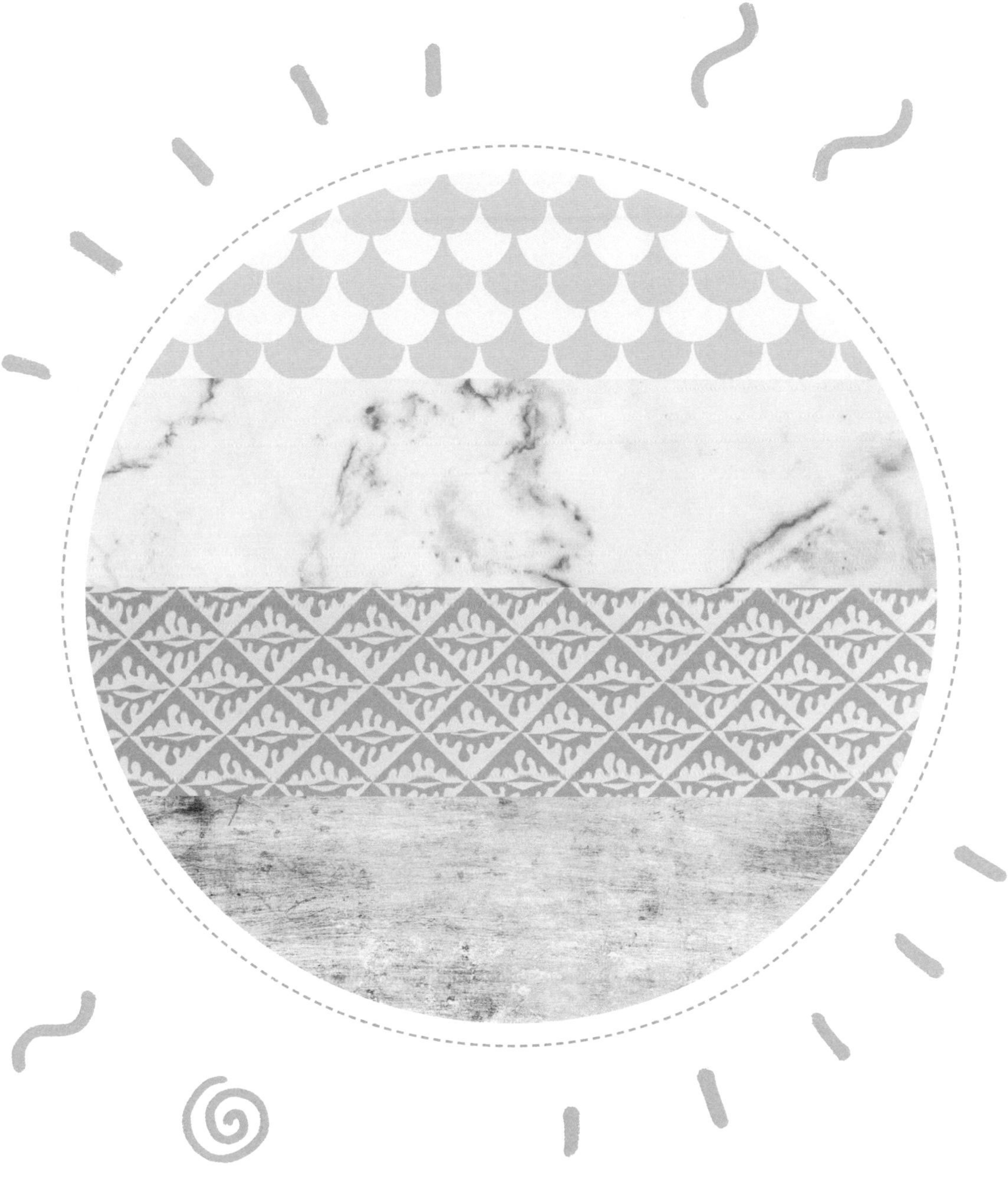

INDEX

Use this space to note your favourite combinations of flavours and ingredients — the beauty of Buddha Bowls is that you can easily invent your own!